Troll Teacher Ideas

TestWise

Primary

Strategies for Success on Standardized Tests

Prepare your children in Grades 1–3 to take nationally normed standardized tests

Eleanor S. Angeles
Edward C. Haggerty

Contents

ISBN: 0-8167-4457-2
Printed in the United States of America
10 9 8 7 6 5 4 3 2 1

The Objectives of *TestWise*

TestWise: Strategies for Success on Standardized Tests is designed to help you prepare your students to take any of the three most common nationally-normed tests: the CAT, or California Achievement Test; the CTBS, or Comprehensive Test of Basic Skills; and the ITBS, the Iowa Test of Basic Skills®.

The most effective way to prepare your students for the reading, math, and study skills content of these standardized tests is to guide your students to do their very best in what you teach them in class. Nothing can replace the day-to-day growth in competence that good teaching fosters. The purpose of *TestWise* is to help you familiarize your students with the formats that standardized tests use and to help them master basic test-taking strategies that will improve their scores and make them more confident and self-assured when they sit down to take the actual test.

To use the strategies and tests in *TestWise* with your students, reproduce the appropriate pages in this book. For added convenience, you may wish to purchase sufficient quantities of *TestWise* to use as a classroom set.

How *TestWise Primary* is Organized

TestWise Primary is divided into nine tests. These tests correspond to the nine skill areas tested on the CAT, the CTBS, and the ITBS. In turn, each of the nine main test sections in *TestWise IPrimary* is divided into two parts:

1. A Set of "Plan and Do" Pages

The two-part "Plan and Do" pages give students experience in answering the kinds of questions that appear on standardized tests. The "Plan" part of each page helps students learn the testing strategies most appropriate for the content of the page. It also reinforces the most beneficial strategies throughout the tests. "Plan" notes are of two kinds, Coach's Corner notes and Student Self-Direction notes.

Coach's Corner Notes

The Coach's Corner notes provide concrete testing tips. The notes aim to help students develop test-taking strategies and avoid the most common test-taking errors. The combination of these two approaches will ensure higher scores, less anxiety, and more confidence.

Student Self-Direction Notes

Special self-directed comments on these pages help make the strategies both real and interactive. They

- model when to use a particular strategy

What are the directions telling me to do?

- explain how to apply a strategy to a particular testing situation

I'll tell myself what the underlined words mean. Then I'll check the answers.

- offer positive self-encouragement

I know I can darken the right circle if I pay attention.

2. **Timed Practice Tests**
   Each of the nine sets of "Plan and Do" pages is followed by a practice test that covers all the areas that students worked on in "Plan and Do." These pages are entitled Timed Practice Test/Use the Strategies on Your Own. You may choose to time these tests or not, as best fits your students' needs. Most standardized tests administered to students in the lower grades impose no time limits. Unless you have an overriding reason to time the tests, you should let your students complete the practice tests at their own pace.
   If you do decide to time the tests, use the times suggested in the chart that follows.

Suggested Times for the Timed Practice Tests

1. Word Analysis	*20 min.*	**6.** Language Usage	*30 min.*
2. Vocabulary	*30 min.*	**7.** Mathematical Computation	*20 min.*
3. Reading Comprehension	*30 min.*	**8.** Mathematical Concepts and Applications	*50 min.*
4. Spelling	*20 min.*	**9.** Reference and Study Skills	*20 min.*
5. Language Mechanics	*15 min.*		

Using the Pages

Answers

Answers are printed on each "Plan and Do" page and Timed Practice Test page. Before duplicating a page, you might want to cover the answers so that they will not print on student copies. You may also leave the answers on the page and have students correct their own work.

The *"Plan and Do"* Pages

Orally go over the sample item at the start of each page. Have students mark in the answer to the sample question and then do the rest of the page. In most cases, third graders will be able to complete the page on their own. Any exceptions are noted in the side columns. You may need to do the pages orally with first and second graders who are less able readers. Read each question and the choices. Then give students time to mark their answers.

After students finish, go over the answers. Invite students to explain how they reached each correct answer. Use the chalkboard or chart paper to record useful strategies your students themselves devise.

The Timed Practice Tests

To replicate test conditions, you should do each end-of-section Timed Practice Test orally with first and second graders. After each Timed Practice Test, go over the answers with your students. Then ask students to discuss how they used the strategies to help them choose their answers.

When to Start

There are thirty-one short "Plan and Do" pages and nine Timed Practice Tests. We recommend starting to use *TestWise* forty to sixty class days before your class is scheduled to take the standardized test your school or school district uses. Keep your *TestWise* work positive and low key. You don't want to inadvertently foster test anxiety in your students.

Planning Notes

Remember to adjust content to match your local curriculum and the grade level of the students you teach. Plan to use only those pages or parts of pages whose content you have already covered in class. You may find especially in the math portions of *TestWise* that you have not yet introduced a skill or concept that *TestWise* covers. In all such cases direct your students to skip the test items you specify. (See examples of Planning Notes on pages 34 and 59.)

A Closer Look at the Standardized Tests

The nationally normed standardized test is a familiar feature of the American educational landscape. No matter whether you support the tests' validity, decry their obtrusiveness, or take the middle ground between these two positions, you want your students to do well on the tests. Your students' success reflects your school's success. Good scores please parents, politicians, and the community at large.

One problem is that students take the CAT, the CTBS, or the ITBS at most only once a year and, in many school districts, less frequently. If you drove your car only once a year, how effective would your driving skills be? If you had to take a road test once a year but never even sat in a car at any other time, how prepared would you feel? In many ways, the annual testing ritual forces young test-takers to face similar obstacles. What can you do to help them perform their best?

Help Your Students Work Smart...

When they prepare for taking the test

Make sure that your students become comfortable and well practiced in applying the proven test-taking strategies in *TestWise*.

Build mastery of test-taking strategies the way you handle reading strategies. Discuss them, remind students to use them, and reinforce how they're used. After a practice test, discuss not just the answers but also the strategies the students used to find them. These follow-up discussions encourage peer coaching, as students learn from one another what strategies they used and how best to implement them. Be open to additional strategies that the students suggest (as long as you believe the strategies will work).

When they interpret directions

One of the key contributors to success on standardized tests is the ability to understand and follow activity directions. Following directions is a skill you can build and reinforce throughout the year. The strategies reminders in *TestWise* will continually tell students to rephrase test directions in their own words and take responsibility for knowing what they are asked to do. You can apply this strategy to all written and oral activity directions you give your students throughout the year.

When they encounter different formats

TestWise gives practice in using all the formats that students will encounter on the newest editions of the major standardized tests. Taking standardized tests is not instinctive. This may be the very first year some children will see a standardized test or, in fact, any kind of multiple-choice test. It takes time and experience to learn how to take this kind of test successfully.

First of all, help students understand what they see. Point out that in *TestWise*, the answer choices have circles in front of them. Don't assume anything. Point out that the empty circle comes before the answer choice. Show that sometimes the answer choices run across the page; sometimes they run down the page; and sometimes they are in columns.

Less able and reluctant readers sometimes don't read all the choices. Encourage students to be thorough. Use the "Plan and Do" pages to point out that there are always four choices.

ITBS Users Only

Of the major tests administered to students in the lower grade levels, only the Iowa Test of Basic Skills does not have students record their answers in their test booklets. Instead, ITBS labels answer choices by letter and uses a separate answer sheet.

Students taking the ITBS need to practice and master additional testing skills. Like all test-takers, they need to find the correct answer. Then they need to transfer that answer onto an answer sheet.

Using the practice answer sheet

You can help students become comfortable with using an answer sheet. On the back of the name grid are nine practice answer grids. A few times before taking the ITBS, have your students practice marking in answers. Begin by darkening in answers at random on your own copy of the answer grid. Then work aloud using a script like this one to dictate your answers: *The answer to item 1 is A. Darken the circle with the letter A inside it. The answer to item 2 is K. Darken the circle with the letter K inside it.* Have each student put a finger on the number of the question he or she is answering on the answer sheet.

Help students notice that the letters J–K–L–M alternate with A–B–C–D inside the circles. Point out how the pattern helps them mark the correct choice in the answer grid. If they go to darken in Ⓐ and find Ⓛ instead, they know they are darkening the wrong circle. It's a clue to check the question number.

When they don't know an answer and want to guess

The Iowa Test of Basic Skills penalizes students for guessing. The CAT and CTBS and many other tests do not. Therefore, depending on the test your students are taking, tell them whether they should guess at an answer or leave a test item blank.

The best strategy for guessing is to eliminate first as many wrong answer choices as possible and then pick the remaining choice that seems more likely to be correct. If none of the answer choices seem incorrect, students taking the ITBS will do better not to guess.

When they experience test anxiety

First, try to forestall test anxiety if you can. Reassure the nervous that they already know how to do everything that's on the test. They don't have to be perfect; they just have to answer the questions they know. Tell them that they'll be learning all sorts of good strategies to help them do well, and express your confidence in them and their abilities.

Don't let your work in *TestWise* be a cause of test anxiety. Be supportive. Help kids stretch. Keep the tone light and don't use the threat of failure on the test as a bludgeon to make students work harder. Reluctance to take practice tests may be due to fear and uncertainty. Do what you must to encourage each student to do his or her best. Learning to take deep breaths also helps students relax.

When tomorrow is testing day

To do their best, students should be well rested and ready to work. Write a note to families encouraging them to make sure their children get a good night's sleep before the test. Families should also make sure that children have a nourishing breakfast on testing day.

If they complete name grids

Name grids are necessary for machine-scoring the tests and reporting the results accurately. But carelessness, anxiety, inattention to detail, and other personal factors cause students to make avoidable mistakes on these forms. Students often darken the wrong circles under their names, put their names or part of their names in the wrong place, and substitute the current year for the year of their birth.

To sidestep mistakes, some teachers fill in the name grids for their classes before they distribute the test booklets. You can also get students accustomed to completing these grids correctly by doing dry runs beforehand and making the activity into a game. Have students develop personal strategies for keeping their place and for putting in the right information. On testing day students will be familiar with these grids and less likely to make careless mistakes. You will find a copy of a name grid and directions on pages 8 and 9 of *TestWise*. Use it for practice.

Completing a Practice Name Grid

To the Teacher

Read these directions aloud. Have the class work with you to fill out a name grid.

A successful start will set a positive tone for the rest of the test. Make sure your students don't get rattled by the name grid, as many do.

Before your students take the actual test, practice completing a name grid.

Strategies

Remind students to use the following strategies:

- Listen carefully
- Put the directions in your own words. Tell yourself what the directions want you to do.
- Use your fingers to keep your place.

Afterwards, have students discuss which strategies worked best for them. Then, as a follow-up, practice completing another name grid in a day or two.

1. Find the words *Last Name* and *First Name*.

- Print your last name in the boxes under the words *last name*. Write one letter in each box. Print your first name in the boxes directly under the words *first name*. If there are not enough spaces for your full name, print as many letters as you can. If your name has a hyphen or an apostrophe, leave it out.
- Now put a finger on the letter you wrote in the first box. Use that finger to go down the column to find the circled letter that matches the letter you wrote in the box. Now darken the circled letter. Do this for each letter in your name. Be sure you darken only one letter in each column.

2. Darken the correct circle for *Male* or *Female*.

3. Write the number of your grade in the box labeled *Grade*. For example, if you are in the third grade, write the number 3.

4. Find the words *Birth Date* and the words *month*, *day*, and *year*.

- Below the word *month* write the name of the month in which you were born. If you were born in May, you would write *May*. Then in the column below, you would darken the circle next to *May*. Now it's your turn. Write the name of the month in which you were born. Darken the circle next to the name of the month.
- Under the word *day* write the number of the day on which you were born. Use a two-number date. If you were born on May 27, you would write the numbers *2* and *7*. If you were born on May 1, you would write the numbers *0* and *1*. Now it's your turn. Write the two numbers that give the date on which you were born. Now below the date you wrote, darken one number in the first column and one number in the second column.
- Under the word *year*, in the space after the number *19*, write the last two numbers of the year in which you were born. Do not write the numbers for *this year*. You were not born this year. If you were born in 1991, you would write *91* in the box. Then you would darken the *9* in the first column and the *1* in the second column. Now it's your turn. Write the last two numbers of the year in which you were born. Now below the number of the year you wrote, darken one number in the first column and one number in the second column.

Last Name										First Name				
Ⓐ	Ⓐ	Ⓐ	Ⓐ	Ⓐ	Ⓐ	Ⓐ	Ⓐ	Ⓐ	Ⓐ	Ⓐ	Ⓐ	Ⓐ	Ⓐ	Ⓐ
Ⓑ	Ⓑ	Ⓑ	Ⓑ	Ⓑ	Ⓑ	Ⓑ	Ⓑ	Ⓑ	Ⓑ	Ⓑ	Ⓑ	Ⓑ	Ⓑ	Ⓑ
Ⓒ	Ⓒ	Ⓒ	Ⓒ	Ⓒ	Ⓒ	Ⓒ	Ⓒ	Ⓒ	Ⓒ	Ⓒ	Ⓒ	Ⓒ	Ⓒ	Ⓒ
Ⓓ	Ⓓ	Ⓓ	Ⓓ	Ⓓ	Ⓓ	Ⓓ	Ⓓ	Ⓓ	Ⓓ	Ⓓ	Ⓓ	Ⓓ	Ⓓ	Ⓓ
Ⓔ	Ⓔ	Ⓔ	Ⓔ	Ⓔ	Ⓔ	Ⓔ	Ⓔ	Ⓔ	Ⓔ	Ⓔ	Ⓔ	Ⓔ	Ⓔ	Ⓔ
Ⓕ	Ⓕ	Ⓕ	Ⓕ	Ⓕ	Ⓕ	Ⓕ	Ⓕ	Ⓕ	Ⓕ	Ⓕ	Ⓕ	Ⓕ	Ⓕ	Ⓕ
Ⓖ	Ⓖ	Ⓖ	Ⓖ	Ⓖ	Ⓖ	Ⓖ	Ⓖ	Ⓖ	Ⓖ	Ⓖ	Ⓖ	Ⓖ	Ⓖ	Ⓖ
Ⓗ	Ⓗ	Ⓗ	Ⓗ	Ⓗ	Ⓗ	Ⓗ	Ⓗ	Ⓗ	Ⓗ	Ⓗ	Ⓗ	Ⓗ	Ⓗ	Ⓗ
Ⓘ	Ⓘ	Ⓘ	Ⓘ	Ⓘ	Ⓘ	Ⓘ	Ⓘ	Ⓘ	Ⓘ	Ⓘ	Ⓘ	Ⓘ	Ⓘ	Ⓘ
Ⓙ	Ⓙ	Ⓙ	Ⓙ	Ⓙ	Ⓙ	Ⓙ	Ⓙ	Ⓙ	Ⓙ	Ⓙ	Ⓙ	Ⓙ	Ⓙ	Ⓙ
Ⓚ	Ⓚ	Ⓚ	Ⓚ	Ⓚ	Ⓚ	Ⓚ	Ⓚ	Ⓚ	Ⓚ	Ⓚ	Ⓚ	Ⓚ	Ⓚ	Ⓚ
Ⓛ	Ⓛ	Ⓛ	Ⓛ	Ⓛ	Ⓛ	Ⓛ	Ⓛ	Ⓛ	Ⓛ	Ⓛ	Ⓛ	Ⓛ	Ⓛ	Ⓛ
Ⓜ	Ⓜ	Ⓜ	Ⓜ	Ⓜ	Ⓜ	Ⓜ	Ⓜ	Ⓜ	Ⓜ	Ⓜ	Ⓜ	Ⓜ	Ⓜ	Ⓜ
Ⓝ	Ⓝ	Ⓝ	Ⓝ	Ⓝ	Ⓝ	Ⓝ	Ⓝ	Ⓝ	Ⓝ	Ⓝ	Ⓝ	Ⓝ	Ⓝ	Ⓝ
Ⓞ	Ⓞ	Ⓞ	Ⓞ	Ⓞ	Ⓞ	Ⓞ	Ⓞ	Ⓞ	Ⓞ	Ⓞ	Ⓞ	Ⓞ	Ⓞ	Ⓞ
Ⓟ	Ⓟ	Ⓟ	Ⓟ	Ⓟ	Ⓟ	Ⓟ	Ⓟ	Ⓟ	Ⓟ	Ⓟ	Ⓟ	Ⓟ	Ⓟ	Ⓟ
Ⓠ	Ⓠ	Ⓠ	Ⓠ	Ⓠ	Ⓠ	Ⓠ	Ⓠ	Ⓠ	Ⓠ	Ⓠ	Ⓠ	Ⓠ	Ⓠ	Ⓠ
Ⓡ	Ⓡ	Ⓡ	Ⓡ	Ⓡ	Ⓡ	Ⓡ	Ⓡ	Ⓡ	Ⓡ	Ⓡ	Ⓡ	Ⓡ	Ⓡ	Ⓡ
Ⓢ	Ⓢ	Ⓢ	Ⓢ	Ⓢ	Ⓢ	Ⓢ	Ⓢ	Ⓢ	Ⓢ	Ⓢ	Ⓢ	Ⓢ	Ⓢ	Ⓢ
Ⓣ	Ⓣ	Ⓣ	Ⓣ	Ⓣ	Ⓣ	Ⓣ	Ⓣ	Ⓣ	Ⓣ	Ⓣ	Ⓣ	Ⓣ	Ⓣ	Ⓣ
Ⓤ	Ⓤ	Ⓤ	Ⓤ	Ⓤ	Ⓤ	Ⓤ	Ⓤ	Ⓤ	Ⓤ	Ⓤ	Ⓤ	Ⓤ	Ⓤ	Ⓤ
Ⓥ	Ⓥ	Ⓥ	Ⓥ	Ⓥ	Ⓥ	Ⓥ	Ⓥ	Ⓥ	Ⓥ	Ⓥ	Ⓥ	Ⓥ	Ⓥ	Ⓥ
Ⓦ	Ⓦ	Ⓦ	Ⓦ	Ⓦ	Ⓦ	Ⓦ	Ⓦ	Ⓦ	Ⓦ	Ⓦ	Ⓦ	Ⓦ	Ⓦ	Ⓦ
Ⓧ	Ⓧ	Ⓧ	Ⓧ	Ⓧ	Ⓧ	Ⓧ	Ⓧ	Ⓧ	Ⓧ	Ⓧ	Ⓧ	Ⓧ	Ⓧ	Ⓧ
Ⓨ	Ⓨ	Ⓨ	Ⓨ	Ⓨ	Ⓨ	Ⓨ	Ⓨ	Ⓨ	Ⓨ	Ⓨ	Ⓨ	Ⓨ	Ⓨ	Ⓨ
Ⓩ	Ⓩ	Ⓩ	Ⓩ	Ⓩ	Ⓩ	Ⓩ	Ⓩ	Ⓩ	Ⓩ	Ⓩ	Ⓩ	Ⓩ	Ⓩ	Ⓩ

Male O
Female O

Grade

Birth Date

MONTH	DAY		YEAR	
			19	
JAN O	⓪	⓪	①	①
FEB O	①	①	②	②
MAR O	②	②	③	③
APR O	③	③	④	④
MAY O		④	⑤	⑤
JUNE O		⑤	⑥	⑥
JULY O		⑥	⑦	⑦
AUG O		⑦	⑧	⑧
SEPT O		⑧	⑨	⑨
OCT O		⑨	⓪	⓪
NOV O				
DEC O				

Troll

TestWise

Primary

Strategies for Success on Standardized Tests

Practice Using an Answer Sheet

TEST 1. Word Analysis

1 Ⓐ Ⓑ Ⓒ Ⓓ	5 Ⓐ Ⓑ Ⓒ Ⓓ	9 Ⓐ Ⓑ Ⓒ Ⓓ	13 Ⓐ Ⓑ Ⓒ Ⓓ	17 Ⓐ Ⓑ Ⓒ Ⓓ
2 Ⓙ Ⓚ Ⓛ Ⓜ	6 Ⓙ Ⓚ Ⓛ Ⓜ	10 Ⓙ Ⓚ Ⓛ Ⓜ	14 Ⓙ Ⓚ Ⓛ Ⓜ	18 Ⓙ Ⓚ Ⓛ Ⓜ
3 Ⓐ Ⓑ Ⓒ Ⓓ	7 Ⓐ Ⓑ Ⓒ Ⓓ	11 Ⓐ Ⓑ Ⓒ Ⓓ	15 Ⓐ Ⓑ Ⓒ Ⓓ	19 Ⓐ Ⓑ Ⓒ Ⓓ
4 Ⓙ Ⓚ Ⓛ Ⓜ	8 Ⓙ Ⓚ Ⓛ Ⓜ	12 Ⓙ Ⓚ Ⓛ Ⓜ	16 Ⓙ Ⓚ Ⓛ Ⓜ	20 Ⓙ Ⓚ Ⓛ Ⓜ

TEST 2. Vocabulary

1 Ⓐ Ⓑ Ⓒ Ⓓ	5 Ⓐ Ⓑ Ⓒ Ⓓ	9 Ⓐ Ⓑ Ⓒ Ⓓ	13 Ⓐ Ⓑ Ⓒ Ⓓ	17 Ⓐ Ⓑ Ⓒ Ⓓ
2 Ⓙ Ⓚ Ⓛ Ⓜ	6 Ⓙ Ⓚ Ⓛ Ⓜ	10 Ⓙ Ⓚ Ⓛ Ⓜ	14 Ⓙ Ⓚ Ⓛ Ⓜ	18 Ⓙ Ⓚ Ⓛ Ⓜ
3 Ⓐ Ⓑ Ⓒ Ⓓ	7 Ⓐ Ⓑ Ⓒ Ⓓ	11 Ⓐ Ⓑ Ⓒ Ⓓ	15 Ⓐ Ⓑ Ⓒ Ⓓ	19 Ⓐ Ⓑ Ⓒ Ⓓ
4 Ⓙ Ⓚ Ⓛ Ⓜ	8 Ⓙ Ⓚ Ⓛ Ⓜ	12 Ⓙ Ⓚ Ⓛ Ⓜ	16 Ⓙ Ⓚ Ⓛ Ⓜ	20 Ⓙ Ⓚ Ⓛ Ⓜ

TEST 3. Reading Comprehension

1 Ⓐ Ⓑ Ⓒ Ⓓ	5 Ⓐ Ⓑ Ⓒ Ⓓ	9 Ⓐ Ⓑ Ⓒ Ⓓ	13 Ⓐ Ⓑ Ⓒ Ⓓ	17 Ⓐ Ⓑ Ⓒ Ⓓ
2 Ⓙ Ⓚ Ⓛ Ⓜ	6 Ⓙ Ⓚ Ⓛ Ⓜ	10 Ⓙ Ⓚ Ⓛ Ⓜ	14 Ⓙ Ⓚ Ⓛ Ⓜ	18 Ⓙ Ⓚ Ⓛ Ⓜ
3 Ⓐ Ⓑ Ⓒ Ⓓ	7 Ⓐ Ⓑ Ⓒ Ⓓ	11 Ⓐ Ⓑ Ⓒ Ⓓ	15 Ⓐ Ⓑ Ⓒ Ⓓ	19 Ⓐ Ⓑ Ⓒ Ⓓ
4 Ⓙ Ⓚ Ⓛ Ⓜ	8 Ⓙ Ⓚ Ⓛ Ⓜ	12 Ⓙ Ⓚ Ⓛ Ⓜ	16 Ⓙ Ⓚ Ⓛ Ⓜ	20 Ⓙ Ⓚ Ⓛ Ⓜ

TEST 4. Spelling

1 Ⓐ Ⓑ Ⓒ Ⓓ	5 Ⓐ Ⓑ Ⓒ Ⓓ	9 Ⓐ Ⓑ Ⓒ Ⓓ	13 Ⓐ Ⓑ Ⓒ Ⓓ	17 Ⓐ Ⓑ Ⓒ Ⓓ
2 Ⓙ Ⓚ Ⓛ Ⓜ	6 Ⓙ Ⓚ Ⓛ Ⓜ	10 Ⓙ Ⓚ Ⓛ Ⓜ	14 Ⓙ Ⓚ Ⓛ Ⓜ	18 Ⓙ Ⓚ Ⓛ Ⓜ
3 Ⓐ Ⓑ Ⓒ Ⓓ	7 Ⓐ Ⓑ Ⓒ Ⓓ	11 Ⓐ Ⓑ Ⓒ Ⓓ	15 Ⓐ Ⓑ Ⓒ Ⓓ	19 Ⓐ Ⓑ Ⓒ Ⓓ
4 Ⓙ Ⓚ Ⓛ Ⓜ	8 Ⓙ Ⓚ Ⓛ Ⓜ	12 Ⓙ Ⓚ Ⓛ Ⓜ	16 Ⓙ Ⓚ Ⓛ Ⓜ	20 Ⓙ Ⓚ Ⓛ Ⓜ

TEST 5. Language Mechanics

1 Ⓐ Ⓑ Ⓒ Ⓓ	5 Ⓐ Ⓑ Ⓒ Ⓓ	9 Ⓐ Ⓑ Ⓒ Ⓓ	13 Ⓐ Ⓑ Ⓒ Ⓓ	17 Ⓐ Ⓑ Ⓒ Ⓓ
2 Ⓙ Ⓚ Ⓛ Ⓜ	6 Ⓙ Ⓚ Ⓛ Ⓜ	10 Ⓙ Ⓚ Ⓛ Ⓜ	14 Ⓙ Ⓚ Ⓛ Ⓜ	18 Ⓙ Ⓚ Ⓛ Ⓜ
3 Ⓐ Ⓑ Ⓒ Ⓓ	7 Ⓐ Ⓑ Ⓒ Ⓓ	11 Ⓐ Ⓑ Ⓒ Ⓓ	15 Ⓐ Ⓑ Ⓒ Ⓓ	19 Ⓐ Ⓑ Ⓒ Ⓓ
4 Ⓙ Ⓚ Ⓛ Ⓜ	8 Ⓙ Ⓚ Ⓛ Ⓜ	12 Ⓙ Ⓚ Ⓛ Ⓜ	16 Ⓙ Ⓚ Ⓛ Ⓜ	20 Ⓙ Ⓚ Ⓛ Ⓜ

TEST 6. Language Usage

1 Ⓐ Ⓑ Ⓒ Ⓓ	5 Ⓐ Ⓑ Ⓒ Ⓓ	9 Ⓐ Ⓑ Ⓒ Ⓓ	13 Ⓐ Ⓑ Ⓒ Ⓓ	17 Ⓐ Ⓑ Ⓒ Ⓓ
2 Ⓙ Ⓚ Ⓛ Ⓜ	6 Ⓙ Ⓚ Ⓛ Ⓜ	10 Ⓙ Ⓚ Ⓛ Ⓜ	14 Ⓙ Ⓚ Ⓛ Ⓜ	18 Ⓙ Ⓚ Ⓛ Ⓜ
3 Ⓐ Ⓑ Ⓒ Ⓓ	7 Ⓐ Ⓑ Ⓒ Ⓓ	11 Ⓐ Ⓑ Ⓒ Ⓓ	15 Ⓐ Ⓑ Ⓒ Ⓓ	19 Ⓐ Ⓑ Ⓒ Ⓓ
4 Ⓙ Ⓚ Ⓛ Ⓜ	8 Ⓙ Ⓚ Ⓛ Ⓜ	12 Ⓙ Ⓚ Ⓛ Ⓜ	16 Ⓙ Ⓚ Ⓛ Ⓜ	20 Ⓙ Ⓚ Ⓛ Ⓜ

TEST 7. Math Computation

1 Ⓐ Ⓑ Ⓒ Ⓓ	5 Ⓐ Ⓑ Ⓒ Ⓓ	9 Ⓐ Ⓑ Ⓒ Ⓓ	13 Ⓐ Ⓑ Ⓒ Ⓓ	17 Ⓐ Ⓑ Ⓒ Ⓓ
2 Ⓙ Ⓚ Ⓛ Ⓜ	6 Ⓙ Ⓚ Ⓛ Ⓜ	10 Ⓙ Ⓚ Ⓛ Ⓜ	14 Ⓙ Ⓚ Ⓛ Ⓜ	18 Ⓙ Ⓚ Ⓛ Ⓜ
3 Ⓐ Ⓑ Ⓒ Ⓓ	7 Ⓐ Ⓑ Ⓒ Ⓓ	11 Ⓐ Ⓑ Ⓒ Ⓓ	15 Ⓐ Ⓑ Ⓒ Ⓓ	19 Ⓐ Ⓑ Ⓒ Ⓓ
4 Ⓙ Ⓚ Ⓛ Ⓜ	8 Ⓙ Ⓚ Ⓛ Ⓜ	12 Ⓙ Ⓚ Ⓛ Ⓜ	16 Ⓙ Ⓚ Ⓛ Ⓜ	20 Ⓙ Ⓚ Ⓛ Ⓜ

TEST 8. Math Concepts and Applications

1 Ⓐ Ⓑ Ⓒ Ⓓ	5 Ⓐ Ⓑ Ⓒ Ⓓ	9 Ⓐ Ⓑ Ⓒ Ⓓ	13 Ⓐ Ⓑ Ⓒ Ⓓ	17 Ⓐ Ⓑ Ⓒ Ⓓ
2 Ⓙ Ⓚ Ⓛ Ⓜ	6 Ⓙ Ⓚ Ⓛ Ⓜ	10 Ⓙ Ⓚ Ⓛ Ⓜ	14 Ⓙ Ⓚ Ⓛ Ⓜ	18 Ⓙ Ⓚ Ⓛ Ⓜ
3 Ⓐ Ⓑ Ⓒ Ⓓ	7 Ⓐ Ⓑ Ⓒ Ⓓ	11 Ⓐ Ⓑ Ⓒ Ⓓ	15 Ⓐ Ⓑ Ⓒ Ⓓ	19 Ⓐ Ⓑ Ⓒ Ⓓ
4 Ⓙ Ⓚ Ⓛ Ⓜ	8 Ⓙ Ⓚ Ⓛ Ⓜ	12 Ⓙ Ⓚ Ⓛ Ⓜ	16 Ⓙ Ⓚ Ⓛ Ⓜ	20 Ⓙ Ⓚ Ⓛ Ⓜ

TEST 9. Reference and Study Skills

1 Ⓐ Ⓑ Ⓒ Ⓓ	5 Ⓐ Ⓑ Ⓒ Ⓓ	9 Ⓐ Ⓑ Ⓒ Ⓓ	13 Ⓐ Ⓑ Ⓒ Ⓓ	17 Ⓐ Ⓑ Ⓒ Ⓓ
2 Ⓙ Ⓚ Ⓛ Ⓜ	6 Ⓙ Ⓚ Ⓛ Ⓜ	10 Ⓙ Ⓚ Ⓛ Ⓜ	14 Ⓙ Ⓚ Ⓛ Ⓜ	18 Ⓙ Ⓚ Ⓛ Ⓜ
3 Ⓐ Ⓑ Ⓒ Ⓓ	7 Ⓐ Ⓑ Ⓒ Ⓓ	11 Ⓐ Ⓑ Ⓒ Ⓓ	15 Ⓐ Ⓑ Ⓒ Ⓓ	19 Ⓐ Ⓑ Ⓒ Ⓓ
4 Ⓙ Ⓚ Ⓛ Ⓜ	8 Ⓙ Ⓚ Ⓛ Ⓜ	12 Ⓙ Ⓚ Ⓛ Ⓜ	16 Ⓙ Ⓚ Ⓛ Ⓜ	20 Ⓙ Ⓚ Ⓛ Ⓜ

Test 1

Word Analysis

Learn and Practice Strategies for Success

1. Recognizing Beginning Sounds

Plan

Listen to the directions. Then put them in your own words. Tell yourself what you need to do.

Darken answer circles completely.

The underlines in the words tell me the sounds to listen for.

Read Aloud

o For Sample A, SAY: stamp…stamp.

o For items 1 to 5, SAY: Darken the circle below the word that begins with the same sound as **1** pole…pole; **2** third…third **3** great…great; **4** spend…spend; **5** drip…drip

Answers: A stand; **1** pot; **2** thank; **3** grow; **4** spot; **5** drill

Do

Darken the circle below the word that begins with the same sound as the word you hear.

Sample A

A	break ○	frozen ○	stand ○

STOP

1	climb ○	pot ○	load ○
2	thank ○	tall ○	base ○
3	grow ○	rain ○	pipe ○
4	share ○	stand ○	spot ○
5	drill ○	bend ○	press ○

STOP

2. Recognizing Ending Sounds

Plan

Find the question you are working on. Put your finger on the number.

Be sure to darken the correct answer circle.

Read Aloud

o For Sample A, SAY: drink…drink.
o For items 1 to 5, SAY: Darken the circle below the word that ends with the same sound as **1** fist…fist; **2** stunt…stunt; **3** third…third; **4** that…that; **5** confess…confess

Answers: **A** pink; **1** list; **2** front; **3** word; **4** sat; **5** less

Do

Darken the circle below the word that ends with the same sound as the word you hear.

Sample A

build ○ hand ○ pink ○

STOP

1 list ○ red ○ smell ○

2 front ○ torn ○ bed ○

3 slam ○ rain ○ word ○

4 sat ○ sad ○ fan ○

5 drop ○ paint ○ less ○

3. Recognizing Compound Words

Plan

Use the sample item to help you know what you need to do.

Be sure to darken the correct answer circle.

Answers: A plane (airplane); **1** foot (barefoot); **2** seed (birdseed); **3** stick (drumstick); **4** cake (cupcake); **5** pan (dustpan); **6** ball (basketball)

Do

Darken the circle below the word that can be added to the underlined word to make a compound word.

Sample A

	<u>air</u>	copy	think	plane
	○	○	○	○

STOP

1	<u>bare</u>	foot	corn	wing
	○	○	○	○
2	<u>bird</u>	hive	seed	steel
	○	○	○	○
3	<u>drum</u>	stick	form	sting
	○	○	○	○
4	<u>cup</u>	plate	seed	cake
	○	○	○	○
5	<u>dust</u>	pan	warm	tab
	○	○	○	○
6	<u>basket</u>	roam	warm	ball
	○	○	○	○

STOP

4. Identifying Root Words

Plan

Remember what important terms mean. The root word is the main word inside the longer word.

Think of your own answer first. Then look in the choices.

Did you change an answer? Erase your old answer completely.

I can find the root word if I tell myself what the bigger word means.

Answers: A freeze; **1** gold; **2** praise; **3** free; **4** thin; **5** friend; **6** repair

Do

Darken the circle below the root word of each underlined word.

Sample A

	<u>freezing</u>	zing	free	freeze
	○	○	○	○
1	<u>golden</u>	old	den	gold
	○	○	○	○
2	<u>praised</u>	raise	praise	is
	○	○	○	○
3	<u>freedom</u>	free	dome	reed
	○	○	○	○
4	<u>thinner</u>	inner	thin	in
	○	○	○	○
5	<u>friendless</u>	end	friend	less
	○	○	○	○
6	<u>repaired</u>	air	red	repair
	○	○	○	○

STOP

Word Analysis

Read Aloud

In this part of the test, you will pick words that have the same beginning sounds as words that you hear.

Put your finger on Sample A.

Read the answer choices carefully. Then darken the circle under the word that has the same beginning sound as date...date.

Give students time to do Sample A on their own. Then explain that both begin with /d/.

Now put your finger on number 1. Darken the circle under the word that begins with the same sound as thin...thin.

For items 2 to 7, SAY

2 chin...chin
3 pebble...pebble
4 twinkle...twinkle
5 crow...crow
6 sell...sell
7 clam...clam

Now put your pencils down.

Answers: A dare; **1** thick; **2** chip; **3** pencil; **4** twice; **5** crate; **6** sandy; **7** clatter

Time (optional): 20 minutes

Sample A

broom ○ bake ○ dare ○

STOP

1 trick ○ tart ○ thick ○

2 bad ○ bring ○ chip ○

3 father ○ pencil ○ stand ○

4 crow ○ thorn ○ twice ○

5 mark ○ crate ○ hurt ○

6 sandy ○ nippy ○ store ○

7 candy ○ clatter ○ picnic ○

Read Aloud

In this part of the test, you will pick words that have the same ending sounds as words that you hear.

Put your finger on Sample B.

Read the answer choices carefully. Then darken the circle under the word that has the same ending sound as quit...quit.

Give students time to do Sample B on their own. Then explain that both end with /t/.

Now put your finger on number 8. Darken the circle under the word that ends with the same sound as cart...cart.

For items 9 to 14, SAY

9 candy...candy
10 sing...sing
11 math...math
12 cement...cement
13 chat...chat
14 sister...sister

Now put your pencils down.

Answers: B flat; **8** heart; **9** handy; **10** ring; **11** cloth; **12** content; **13** flat; **14** master

Sample B

	sandy ○	flat ○	calm ○

STOP

8	string ○	heart ○	fret ○
9	thick ○	push ○	handy ○
10	sink ○	sort ○	ring ○
11	cloth ○	grid ○	upset ○
12	part ○	content ○	disk ○
13	fast ○	flat ○	stand ○
14	standing ○	remind ○	master ○

Read Aloud

In this part of the test, you will pick words that can be added to the underlined words to make compound words.

Put your finger on Sample C.

Read the underlined word and the answer choices carefully. Then darken the circle below the word that can be added to the underlined word to make a compound word.

Give students time to do Sample C on their own. Then explain that fire *and* place *can be written together to make a compound word,* fireplace.

Now put your finger on number 15. Do numbers 15 to 21 in the same way we did Sample C.

Work until you reach the stop sign at the bottom of the page. Then put your pencils down.

Begin now.

Answers: C place (fireplace); **15** paper (newspaper); **16** lace (shoelace); **17** coat (raincoat); **18** work (homework); **19** room (schoolroom); **20** beat (drumbeat); **21** boat (rowboat)

Sample C

	fire	sing	place	mirror
	○	○	○	○

STOP

15	news	saw	paper	dinner
	○	○	○	○
16	shoe	gift	honor	lace
	○	○	○	○
17	rain	sun	coat	thumb
	○	○	○	○
18	home	work	half	stare
	○	○	○	○
19	school	cloud	room	thanks
	○	○	○	○
20	drum	beat	dome	drink
	○	○	○	○
21	row	sail	boat	bird
	○	○	○	○

Read Aloud

In this part of the test, you will pick words that are the root words of longer words.

Put your finger on Sample D.

Read the underlined word and the answer choices carefully. Then darken the circle below the word that is the root word of the word that is underlined.

Give students time to do Sample D on their own. Then explain that driver *is the root word of* driverless. *Explain that the word means "without a driver."*

Now put your finger on number 22. Do numbers 22 to 28 in the same way we did Sample D.

Work until you reach the stop sign at the bottom of the page. Then put your pencils down.

Begin now.

Answers: D driver; **22** thought; **23** boil; **24** float; **25** crowd; **26** deliver; **27** favor; **28** power

Sample D

	driverless	river	driver	less
	○	○	○	○

STOP

22	thoughtful	ought	thought	full
	○	○	○	○
23	boiler	oil	boil	oiler
	○	○	○	○
24	floating	float	oat	ting
	○	○	○	○
25	crowded	row	crow	crowd
	○	○	○	○
26	delivery	liver	live	deliver
	○	○	○	○
27	favorable	favor	or	able
	○	○	○	○
28	overpowering	ring	power	pow
	○	○	○	○

Test 2

Vocabulary Learn and Practice Strategies for Success

5. Identifying Words with Similar Meanings

Plan

Tell yourself what you need to do. Put the directions in your own words.

First tell yourself what the underlined word means. Then look at the choices.

Darken answer circles completely.

Good for me!
I can do this.

Answers: A clean; **1** box; **2** fall; **3** story; **4** soft; **5** pound

Do

Darken the circle next to the word that has the same or almost the same meaning as the underlined word.

Sample A

wipe the table

○ build ○ cover
○ clean ○ leave

STOP

1 heavy carton

○ box ○ shelf
○ load ○ post

2 in autumn

○ winter ○ fall
○ summer ○ spring

3 tell a tale

○ friend ○ secret
○ story ○ goal

4 gentle breeze

○ rainy ○ strong
○ soft ○ wintery

5 hammer nails

○ drill ○ bend
○ pound ○ loosen

STOP

6. Identifying Words with Opposite Meanings

Plan

Tell yourself what you need to do. Put the directions in your own words.

Read all the answers before you pick.

Skip questions you can't answer. Come back to them later.

Stay focused. Watch out for choices that are meant to throw you off track.

I can go back and check my work.

Answers: A tiny; **1** dry; **2** under; **3** thin; **4** wide; **5** kind

Do

Darken the circle next to the word or phrase that has the opposite meaning of each underlined word or phrase.

Sample A

gigantic tree

- ○ bare
- ○ tall
- ○ tiny
- ○ green

STOP

1 damp clothes

- ○ wet
- ○ dry
- ○ colorful
- ○ ironed

2 on top of the rug

- ○ near
- ○ above
- ○ under
- ○ beside

3 thick sandwich

- ○ thin
- ○ fatty
- ○ round
- ○ tasty

4 narrow hallway

- ○ upstairs
- ○ straight
- ○ clean
- ○ wide

5 nasty remark

- ○ mean
- ○ kind
- ○ loud
- ○ short

STOP

7. Understanding Prefixes and Suffixes

Plan

Tell yourself what you need to do. Put the directions in your own words.

Think about the example words. Tell yourself what they mean.

Prefixes and suffixes change what a word means.

Answers: A not; **1** again; **2** like; **3** can be; **4** covered with; **5** one who

Do

Darken the circle next to the word or phrase that best gives the meaning of the underlined prefix or suffix.

Sample A

unseen   unhappy

○ very   ○ under
○ with   ○ not

STOP

1 recheck   reread

○ after   ○ again
○ under   ○ before

2 childish   foolish

○ near   ○ can be
○ like   ○ beside

3 repairable   doable

○ can be   ○ one who
○ like   ○ in the manner of

4 cloudy   dirty

○ upstairs   ○ straight
○ clean   ○ covered with

5 thinker   teacher

○ with   ○ one who
○ toward   ○ without

8. Using Words with More Than One Meaning

Plan

Tell yourself what you need to do. Put the directions in your own words.

Try each word in both sentences.

Erase your old answer completely if you change your mind.

Does the sentence make sense with the new word in it?

Answers: A hand; **1** cold; **2** pen; **3** note; **4** gobble; **5** light

Do

Darken the circle next to the word that fits in both of the sentences.

Sample A

Please _____ me your dish.
Put your _____ in that glove.

○ give ○ bring
○ hand ○ throw

STOP

---

1 Very _____ weather makes me shiver.
Wear a coat, or you'll catch a _____.

○ hazy ○ sick
○ chilly ○ cold

---

2 The lamb escaped from its _____.
Bring a _____ or a pencil to school.

○ paper ○ pen
○ field ○ marker

---

3 I read the _____ from my best friend.
I cannot read a _____ of music.

○ note ○ piano
○ paper ○ song

---

4 Don't _____ your food.
I heard the _____ of a wild turkey.

○ call ○ forget
○ clean ○ gobble

---

5 A _____ color shows the dirt easily.
We forgot to _____ the fire in the fireplace.

○ light ○ bright
○ burn ○ pale

STOP

9. Completing Sentences

Plan

Remember to put the directions in your own words.

See how the format changes. There's a sentence with a blank in it. Then there's a question about the sentence.

Make sure you darken the correct circle. Don't put your answer in the wrong place.

I have to read the sentence before I pick a word.

Answers: A construct; **1** defeated; **2** flameproof; **3** hazardous; **4** lyrics; **5** stubborn

Do

Darken the circle next to the word that best completes the sentence.

Sample A

The children used blocks to _____ a tower.
Which word means the children built a tower?

○ neglect ○ conduct
○ construct ○ erase

STOP

---

1 Our soccer team _____ the Cougars.
Which word means that the team beat the Cougars?

○ cheered ○ congratulated
○ respected ○ defeated

---

2 These curtains are _____.
Which word means that the curtains will not catch fire?

○ neat ○ correct
○ flameproof ○ waterproof

---

3 The storm made the trip home _____.
Which word means that the trip was dangerous?

○ hazardous ○ grumbling
○ unhurt ○ damaged

---

4 Jeff's sister knows the _____ to every new song.
Which word means the words to the songs?

○ beat ○ lyrics
○ dance ○ notes

---

5 The _____ child made a loud fuss.
Which word means that the child would not give in?

○ sloppy ○ unkind
○ stubborn ○ unhappy

STOP

Vocabulary

Time (optional): 30 minutes

Read Aloud

In this part of the test, you will pick words that have similar meanings.

Put your finger on Sample A.

Read the phrase and the answer choices carefully. Then darken the circle next to the word that has the *same* or *almost the same meaning* as the underlined word.

Give students time to do Sample A on their own. Then explain that to obey rules and to follow rules mean the same thing.

Now put your finger on number 1. Do numbers 1 to 6 in the same way we did Sample A.

Work until you reach the stop sign at the bottom of the page. Then put your pencils down.

Begin now.

Answers: A follow; **1** yell; **2** end; **3** gift; **4** smooth; **5** smart; **6** run

Sample A

<u>obey</u> rules

- ○ find
- ○ follow
- ○ hate
- ○ make

STOP

---

1 loudly <u>shout</u>

- ○ yell
- ○ beg
- ○ hide
- ○ walk

2 <u>finish</u> the story

- ○ start
- ○ tell
- ○ enjoy
- ○ end

3 a fancy <u>present</u>

- ○ now
- ○ gift
- ○ money
- ○ pain

4 <u>calm</u> water

- ○ rough
- ○ stale
- ○ smooth
- ○ clear

5 <u>bright</u> idea

- ○ smart
- ○ dull
- ○ unclear
- ○ steady

6 <u>scurry</u> home

- ○ stay
- ○ run
- ○ visit
- ○ see

STOP

Read Aloud

In this part of the test, you will pick words that have opposite meanings.

Put your finger on Sample B.

Read the phrase and the answer choices carefully. Then darken the circle next to the word that has the opposite meaning of the underlined word.

Give students time to do Sample B on their own. Then explain that the opposite of a weak leader is a strong leader.

Now put your finger on number 7. Do numbers 7 to 12 in the same way we did Sample B.

Work until you reach the stop sign at the bottom of the page. Then put your pencils down.

Begin now.

Answers: B strong; **7** sick; **8** cry; **9** asleep; **10** wild; **11** light; **12** straight

Sample B

weak leader

- ○ new
- ○ wild
- ○ strong
- ○ sick

STOP

7 healthy pet

- ○ new
- ○ lost
- ○ loved
- ○ sick

8 laugh loudly

- ○ run
- ○ pour
- ○ fill
- ○ cry

9 wide awake

- ○ friendly
- ○ dull
- ○ asleep
- ○ calm

10 tame animals

- ○ wild
- ○ small
- ○ cute
- ○ heavy

11 dark colors

- ○ powerful
- ○ gray
- ○ light
- ○ gloomy

12 crooked road

- ○ straight
- ○ dirty
- ○ clean
- ○ broken

STOP

Read Aloud

In this part of the test, you will pick the meaning of a prefix or a suffix used in a word.

Put your finger on Sample C.

Read the example words and the answer choices carefully. Then darken the circle next to the word or phrase that gives the best meaning of the prefix or suffix underlined in the example words.

Give students time to do Sample C on their own. Then explain that dis- *means "not" or "the opposite of." Thus,* disagree *means that you do not agree. A* dishonest person *is a person who is not honest.*

Now put your finger on number 13. Do numbers 13 to 18 in the same way we did Sample C.

Work until you reach the stop sign at the bottom of the page. Then put your pencils down.

Begin now.

Answers: C not; **13** the opposite of; **14** every; **15** having; **16** without; **17** the opposite of; **18** full of

Sample C

disagree   dishonest

- ○ again
- ○ not
- ○ with
- ○ against

STOP

13 nonworking   nonpaying

- ○ before
- ○ very
- ○ the opposite of
- ○ like

14 hourly   weekly

- ○ every
- ○ against
- ○ one who
- ○ the state of

15 wealthy   squeaky

- ○ more
- ○ toward
- ○ without
- ○ having

16 hopeless   blameless

- ○ without
- ○ every
- ○ having
- ○ the state of

17 disrespect   disobey

- ○ very
- ○ into
- ○ the opposite of
- ○ the state of

18 glorious   mountainous

- ○ not
- ○ full of
- ○ without
- ○ every

Read Aloud

In this part of the test, you will pick words that have more than one meaning.

Put your finger on Sample D.

Read the sentences and the answer choices carefully. Then darken the circle next to the word that fits in both sentences.

Give students time to do Sample D on their own. Then explain that bill *meaning "a piece of paper money" fits the meaning of the first sentence and* bill *meaning "a part of a bird's jaw" fits the meaning of the second sentence.*

Now put your finger on number 19. Do numbers 19 to 24 in the same way we did Sample D.

Work until you reach the stop sign at the bottom of the page. Then put your pencils down.

Begin now.

Answers: D bill; **19** punch; **20** pass; **21** saw; **22** leaves; **23** fresh; **24** gum

Sample D

I found a five-dollar _____ on the sidewalk.
A duck has a flat _____ and webbed feet.

○ wing ○ back
○ bill ○ short

STOP

19 Everyone at the party drank fruit _____.
The bully started to _____ my arm.

○ hurt ○ punch
○ juice ○ hit

20 Every student needs a _____ to leave the room.
Hundreds of cars _____ here every day.

○ run ○ return
○ pass ○ permit

21 A sharp _____ can cut wood easily.
Who _____ the sunset yesterday?

○ noticed ○ tool
○ liked ○ saw

22 The wind will blow away the _____ from the tree.
The bus to the city _____ at noon.

○ branches ○ stops
○ leaves ○ goes

23 This tomato is very _____ and tasty.
A _____ remark got me into trouble.

○ fresh ○ silly
○ nasty ○ rude

24 My _____ bled when my tooth fell out.
I must not chew _____ in school.

○ lip ○ gum
○ mouth ○ candy

STOP

Read Aloud

In this part of the test, you will pick words that complete sentences. You will pick the word that best fits the meaning of the sentence.

Put your finger on Sample E.

Read the sentence, the question, and the answer choices carefully. Then darken the circle next to the word that best completes the sentence.

Give students time to do Sample E on their own. Then explain that blazing *is another word for* burning. *The word* blazing *fits the meaning of the sentence.*

Now put your finger on number 25. Do numbers 25 to 30 in the same way we did Sample E.

Work until you reach the stop sign at the bottom of the page. Then put your pencils down.

Begin now.

Answers: E blazing; **25** growled; **26** hectic; **27** recall; **28** rematch; **29** gigantic; **30** pasture

Sample E

The _____ sun hurt my eyes.
Which word means burning?

○ calm ○ blazing
○ tidy ○ timid

STOP

25 The dogs _____ at each other.
Which word means the dogs made deep, low, angry sounds?

○ new ○ lost
○ growled ○ sick

26 The last day before our big trip was very _____.
Which word means that the day was wildly busy?

○ calm ○ fearful
○ hectic ○ windy

27 Amanda tried to _____ when the accident happened.
Which word means that she tried to remember?

○ recall ○ repeat
○ invite ○ foretell

28 The game was a tie, and the team wanted a _____.
Which word means the team wanted to play another game?

○ point ○ rematch
○ report ○ remedy

29 The class drew a _____ poster for the food drive.
Which word means that the poster was very large?

○ gloomy ○ light-hearted
○ clever ○ gigantic

30 The horses grazed in the _____.
Which word names a place where horses can eat grass?

○ saddle ○ pasture
○ hoof ○ harness

STOP

10. Matching Pictures and Sentences

Plan

Remember to put the directions in your own words. Tell yourself what you need to do.

Look at each picture first.
Tell yourself what is happening.

Next, read all the answer choices.
Then pick the best one.

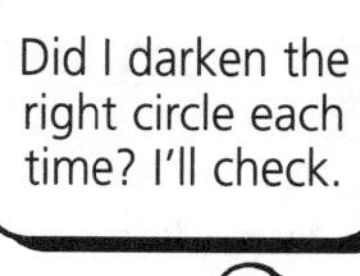

Did I darken the right circle each time? I'll check.

That arrow must mean that there are more questions on the next page.

Answers: A Kira is playing with her yo-yo.
1 Dad is putting the clothes into the washer.
2 Lisa is flying her kite in the park.
3 Sam is kicking a soccer ball.

Do

Darken the circle next to the sentence that tells about the picture.

Sample A

○ Kira is climbing a tree.
○ Kira is playing with her yo-yo.
○ Kira is watching her baby sister.

1

○ Dad is changing a lightbulb.
○ Dad is washing the car.
○ Dad is putting the clothes into the washer.

2

○ Lisa is flying her kite in the park.
○ Liz is watching Lisa swim.
○ Lisa is tying her shoe.

3

○ Sam is eating lunch.
○ Sam is kicking a soccer ball.
○ Sam is walking his dog.

GO ON

Put your finger on number 4 on this page.

If you can't answer a question, skip it. Come back to it later.

I'm getting good at this!

Answers: 4 Alice is swimming in the pool. **5** My sister is feeding the dog. **6** Tom is racing Jonah across the field. **7** Seth is sweeping the floor.

4

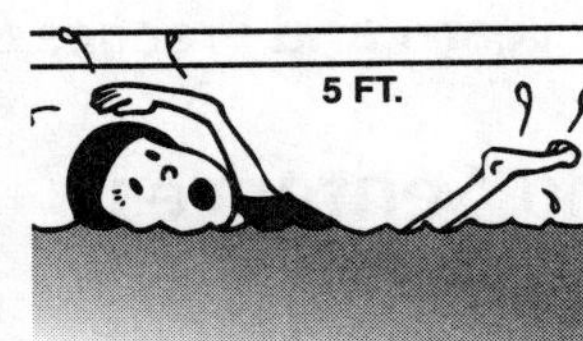
5 FT.

- ○ Alice is swimming in the pool.
- ○ Alice is drying her hair.
- ○ Alice is reading a book.

5

- ○ My sister is washing her hands.
- ○ My sister is drying dishes.
- ○ My sister is feeding the dog.

6

- ○ Tom is building a bridge with blocks.
- ○ Tom is racing Jonah across the field.
- ○ Tom is on his hands and knees.

7

- ○ Seth is sweeping the floor.
- ○ Seth is playing a video game.
- ○ Seth is watching a movie.

STOP

11. Reading Stories

Plan

Read for a purpose.

First read the questions that come after the story. Read just the questions. Skip the answer choices.

Then read the story. Look for answers to those questions. Put the answers in your own words.

Next go back to the questions. Read all the answer choices. Find the answer that is most like your answer. Darken the circle next to it.

I'll really pay attention when I read.

To the Teacher *Please see the Planning Notes on pages 33, 34, and 39.*

Answers: A Its fur looks like calico cloth. **1** They were work animals. **2** It can learn many commands.

Do

Read the story. Darken the circle next to the correct answer.

Sample A

The black, brown, and orange patches of fur on a white background that make this cat so interesting to lookat also gave the Calico its name. "Calico" is a kind of cloth that is spotted with many bright colors–just as this cat is.

How did the Calico cat get its name?

- ○ Its fur is made of cloth.
- ○ Its fur is short.
- ○ Its fur looks like calico cloth.
- ○ It is a playful cat.

Many years ago, horses were important farm animals. Before people had trucks and other machines, farmers used horses to pull plows and do other work. Today, most farm horses are ridden for fun.

A horse's body helps it run for long periods of time. Its legs are long and strong, so it can run quickly. It has wide nostrils and large, powerful lungs to help it breathe easily. A horse is also smart enough to learn many commands.

1 Why were horses important long ago?

- ○ They were pets.
- ○ Children loved them.
- ○ They were work animals.
- ○ They ran farm machines.

2 What tells you that a horse is an intelligent animal?

- ○ Large nostrils help it breathe easily.
- ○ It can learn many commands.
- ○ It can run for long periods of time.
- ○ Its legs are long.

GO ON

Stay focused. Watch out for choices that are meant to throw you off track.

I'll keep my finger on the number of the question I'm working on.

A tiger's stripes do more than make it look beautiful. They also help the tiger hide in the long grass, so it can sneak up on its prey. Stripes also help us tell one tiger from another. No two tigers have the same pattern of stripes.

Tigers like to be by themselves. The only tigers that live together are a mother and her cubs, or babies. A tiger usually has 2-4 cubs. The cubs start learning how to hunt when they are about six months old. But they will stay with their mother for several years.

3 How can people tell two tigers in the wild apart?

○ by their stripes
○ by their names
○ by the way they hunt
○ by the way they raise cubs

4 When do tigers begin to learn how to hunt?

○ when they have cubs
○ when they are about six months old
○ when they are several years old
○ when they are 2 to 4 years old

Every fall, Monarch butterflies go on a fantastic journey. They leave their homes in Canada and the northern United States and fly south to California, Florida, Texas, and Mexico, where it is warmer. When spring comes again, the Monarchs migrate back north. This trip can be as long as 2,000 miles (3,220 kilometers)!

As the Monarchs fly north, they lay eggs on the milkweed plant. These eggs hatch into caterpillars. As the caterpillars grow, their skins become too small for them and have to be shed. This is called molting.

5 How far might Monarch butterflies fly when they migrate?

○ 100 miles
○ 200 miles
○ 2,000 miles
○ 20,000 miles

6 When do Monarch butterflies migrate south?

○ every two years
○ every fall
○ every spring
○ only when they are born

GO ON

Answers: 3 by their stripes; **4** when they are about six months old; **5** 2,000 miles; **6** every fall

Most of the time, a porcupine chews the bark off of trees. It is quiet and doesn't bother anyone. But if a porcupine is attacked, it has a very interesting way of defending itself. Its thick fur is covered with strong, sharp quills. These quills are very lightly attached to the porcupine's skin and have tiny hooks, called barbs, on the ends. If an attacker is hit by the porcupine's tail or touches the porcupine's body—ouch! The quills stick in the attacker's skin.

In the spring, a mother porcupine moves into a hollow log or a pile of branches and leaves. There she has a baby. The baby is born with all its quills.

I can look back in the story if I don't remember an answer.

7 What does a porcupine use to defend itself?

- ○ bark from trees
- ○ its fur
- ○ its quills
- ○ its sharp claws

8 Why do a porcupine's quills have barbs?

- ○ The barbs help the porcupine climb trees.
- ○ The barbs help the porcupine find food.
- ○ The barbs keep baby porcupines from hurting their mother.
- ○ The barbs help the quills stick in an attacker's skin.

PLANNING NOTE

Tell students to stop at the bottom of this page if you do not want them to read and answer questions about the long passage on page 34.

Most newborn baby birds are covered with soft furry down. Their eyes are usually open. By the end of the day they are able to feed themselves, run around, or swim with their parents.

But some birds, such as woodpeckers, parrots, and hawks, are born blind and helpless. They must stay in the nest until they can open their eyes and move around. During this time, their parents feed and protect them.

9 How soon can most newborn baby birds feed themselves?

- ○ by the end of the first week
- ○ after two days
- ○ by the end of the first day
- ○ as soon as they hatch

10 Why are some young birds very helpless?

- ○ Their parents do not feed them.
- ○ They do not have wings.
- ○ They cannot eat.
- ○ They are born with their eyes closed.

Answers: 7 its quills; **8** The barbs help the quills stick in an attacker's skin. **9** by the end of the first day; **10** They are born with their eyes closed.

GO ON

PLANNING NOTE

The long passage and questions on pages 34 and 35 are appropriate mainly for older, experienced readers or students who will take the ITBS. At grade 3 and below, the CAT and CTBS do not use long passages.

You may wish to have your students skip pages 34 and 35.

Remember to read the questions *before* you read the story.

I can go back and check my work.

Do you need plenty of special equipment to play basketball? Not at all! Basketball players need practically no special equipment. They usually wear just shorts, sleeveless shirts, and sneakers.

Sometimes people play or practice basketball in regular street shoes. However, it is always best to wear sneakers. Buy the best sneakers you can afford if you are very serious about basketball. Make sure they fit right and provide strong ankle support.

The most important things you need for a basketball game are a basketball and a special place to play. That place must be a flat, level area. It can be inside a gym. During warm weather, it can be outside at a school or playground. It can even be your own driveway or backyard. In basketball, that area is called a court. A court is usually in the shape of a rectangle, and has long side boundaries and shorter end boundaries.

At the ends of a basketball court are goals, although some games can be played with just one goal. A basketball goal is made up of two parts. One part is a flat, smooth backboard section. It is usually rectangular and made of wood, metal, or thick glass.

The second part is the goal itself, usually called the "basket." The goal is a circle of iron attached to the backboard. It is also called the hoop or the rim. It sticks out from the backboard so the ball can be shot through it. A net is attached on the bottom of the rim. (Some outdoor goals have no nets.) Basketball goals are always hung above the court. The ball must be shot up into them.

The object of a basketball game is to score more points than the other team. Points are scored by shooting the ball into the basket. Under normal conditions, each goal in basketball is worth two points. That is called a field goal.

GO ON

In this kind of test, the questions are about the story. To answer these questions,

- DON'T use everything you know about basketball.
- DO use only what the story tells you.

I can go back and check my answers against the story.

Answers: 11 a basketball and a place to play; **12** sneakers; **13** flat and level; **14** a court; **15** a basket; **16** the backboard; **17** Your side scores more points than the other side. **18** two points

11 What do you need to play basketball?

- ○ a coach and a full team
- ○ lots of special gear
- ○ a basketball and a place to play
- ○ helmets and special shoes

12 What are the best shoes to wear when you play basketball?

- ○ boots
- ○ sneakers
- ○ slippers
- ○ cleats

13 Which words tell what a basketball court must be?

- ○ indoors and warm
- ○ inside a gym
- ○ flat and level
- ○ drafty and cold

14 What is the area in which you play basketball called?

- ○ a court
- ○ an area
- ○ a field
- ○ a rink

15 What is the special name for the goal in basketball?

- ○ a shot
- ○ a birdie
- ○ a run
- ○ a basket

16 What holds the hoop up?

- ○ the net
- ○ the school yard
- ○ the rim
- ○ the backboard

17 How do you win a game of basketball?

- ○ The referee tells you that you won.
- ○ Your side scores more points than the other side
- ○ The crowd picks the winner.
- ○ The teams flip a coin.

18 Under normal conditions, how many points is a goal in basketball worth?

- ○ no points
- ○ one point
- ○ two points
- ○ three points

12. Deciding What Could Not Happen

Plan

Remember to put the directions in your own words.

Think about Sample A. How does it help you understand what to do?

Read all the answers first. Then pick the best one. Remember, three of the four things <u>can</u> happen.

If I change an answer, I'll erase everything in the circle.

Answers: A Two birds in an airplane flew in. **1** A tree walked by with an umbrella. **2** The basket bent over and caught the ball. **3** The crayons sneaked out of the crayon box. **4** The telephone floated gently through the air.

Do

Darken the circle next to the sentence that tells something that could <u>not</u> happen in real life.

Sample A

- ○ Dinner was cooking on the stove.
- ○ Two birds in an airplane flew in.
- ○ The dog sat next to the table.
- ○ The dog begged for food.

1
- ○ Storm clouds filled the sky.
- ○ Lightning hit a tree.
- ○ A tree walked by with an umbrella.
- ○ The river flooded the land.

2
- ○ Three boys played basketball.
- ○ Harry threw the ball very hard.
- ○ Harry missed the basket.
- ○ The basket bent over and caught the ball.

3
- ○ The crayons sneaked out of the crayon box.
- ○ Anne drew a sunset.
- ○ Chris drew a beach party.
- ○ Ted liked to use colored pencils.

4
- ○ The phone call was for me.
- ○ The telephone floated gently through the air.
- ○ Grandma invited us to her house.
- ○ Mom drove us there in the car.

Reading Comprehension

Time (optional): 30 minutes

Read Aloud

In this part of the test, you will match pictures and sentences.

Put your finger on Sample A.

Study each picture and read the answer choices carefully. Then darken the circle next to the sentence that tells about the picture.

Give students time to do Sample A on their own. Then explain that the picture shows a girl riding on a skateboard. The picture thus matches the sentence "Linda is riding on her skateboard."

Now put your finger on number 1. Do numbers 1 to 8 in the same way we did Sample A.

When you get to the bottom of this page, go on to the next page. Work until you reach the stop sign at the bottom of the next page. Then put your pencils down.

Begin now.

Answers: A Linda is riding on her skateboard. **1** Kevin is mowing the lawn. **2** Mandy's hat blew off. **3** Jason tripped on a small rock.

Sample A

- ○ Linda is eating ice cream.
- ○ Linda is riding on her skateboard.
- ○ Linda is playing the violin.

1

- ○ Kevin is mowing the lawn.
- ○ Kevin is writing a letter.
- ○ Kevin and Bill are raking leaves.

2

- ○ Mandy leaned over the water fountain
- ○ Mandy saw a rabbit.
- ○ Mandy's hat blew off.

3

- ○ Jason dipped his hand into the stream.
- ○ Jason tripped on a small rock.
- ○ Jason picked flowers in the woods.

4

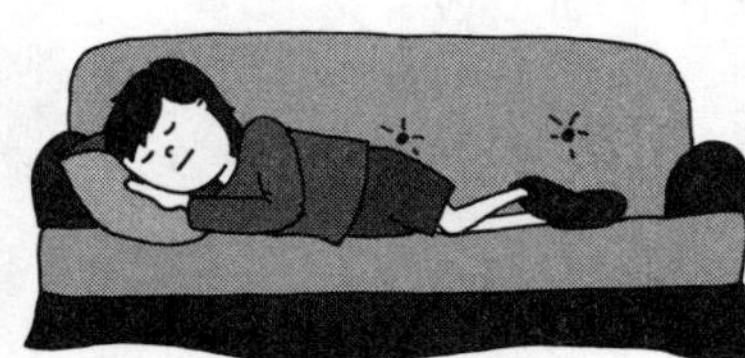

- ○ Mary went to school all day.
- ○ Mary is reading a book.
- ○ Mary is asleep on the sofa.

5

- ○ Mark is swimming in the lake.
- ○ Mark is paddling a canoe.
- ○ Mark is hiking along the shore of the lake.

6

- ○ Carlos is blowing up a balloon.
- ○ Carlos is wrapping her sister's birthday gift.
- ○ Carlos is writing thank-you notes to guests.

7

- ○ Don is writing a postcard.
- ○ Don is cleaning his room.
- ○ Don is taking a photograph.

8

- ○ Luke is helping Mary wash the car.
- ○ Luke and Mary are building a tree house.
- ○ Mary is helping Luke feed the stray cat.

STOP

Answers: 4 Mary is asleep on the sofa. **5** Mark is paddling a canoe. **6** Carlos is blowing up a balloon. **7** Don is taking a photograph. **8** Luke and Mary are building a tree house.

Read Aloud

In this part of the test, you will answer questions about reading passages.

Put your finger on Sample B.

Read the passage, the questions, and the answer choices carefully. Then darken the circle next to the correct answer.

Give students time to do Sample B on their own. Then explain that a Scottish Fold, as the last sentence states, is a breed of cat.

Now put your finger on number 9. Do numbers 9 to 18 (or 9 to 26) in the same way we did Sample B.

Work until you reach the stop sign at the bottom of page 41 (or 43). Then put your pencils down.

Begin now.

PLANNING NOTE

If you omitted the long passage and questions on pages 34–35, you may also wish to have students omit the long passage and questions on pages 42–43. Have students cross out GO ON on the bottom of page 41 and write in STOP.

Answers: B a breed of cat; **9** on large farms, as food; **10** a rooster

Sample B

In 1961, a cat was found in Scotland whose ears folded forward and down. Soon, more of these cats were born, and the Scottish Fold became a new breed of cat. It is one of the newest breeds.

What is a Scottish Fold?

- ○ a clothing style
- ○ a food
- ○ a breed of cat
- ○ a dog

A chicken is a special kind of bird that gives us meat and eggs to eat. Like cattle, chickens are very important farm animals. Long ago, chickens were kept on farms to help feed the farmer's family. Today, most chickens are raised on very large farms. Some of these farms have millions of chickens!

The male chicken is called a rooster. It has a bright red comb on the top of its head and red wattles hanging down from its beak. Female chickens, called hens, lay many eggs each day. Some of these eggs are special—they have tiny baby chicks inside them! Farmers do not bring these eggs to the market.

9 How are most chickens raised today?

- ○ on small farms, as pets
- ○ on small farms, as food
- ○ on large farms, as food
- ○ on cattle farms, as family food

10 What is another name for a male chicken?

- ○ a hen
- ○ a chick
- ○ a rooster
- ○ a market

GO ON

Unlike most cats, lions like to be with one another. They live together in groups called prides. A pride is a family group that includes several adult males, adult females (called lionesses), and a number of young cubs. Male cubs stay with a pride until they are two or three years old. Then the adults chase them away. In time, the young lions will be strong enough to lead prides of their own.

11 What is a pride of lions?

- ○ a family group of lions
- ○ a group of cubs
- ○ lions in a zoo
- ○ a group of female lions with cubs

12 Why do male cubs leave the pride at age two or three?

- ○ They cannot catch food.
- ○ They refuse to eat.
- ○ The adults chase them away.
- ○ They want to be cubs again.

How can you tell a moth from a butterfly? There are four ways. The best clue is the time. Butterflies are active during the day, but moths come out at night. The other differences are in their bodies. Most butterflies have thin antennae with knobs on the end, and thin, hairless bodies. Moths often have thick, feathery antennae, and their bodies are fat and furry. They also spread their wings out when they are resting, while butterflies hold their wings up in the air.

The Luna moth is often seen in the eastern part of the United States. Its pale green color and long wings make this one of the prettiest moths.

13 When are butterflies active?

- ○ during the day
- ○ at night
- ○ only in the very early morning
- ○ on rainy days

14 What is true about moths?

- ○ They do not have antennae.
- ○ Their antennae are thick and feathery.
- ○ They are not able to fly.
- ○ They have thin, hairless bodies.

GO ON

Answers: 11 a family group of lions; **12** The adults chase them away; **13** during the day; **14** Their antennae are thick and feathery.

When opossums are born, they are so small that 20 could fit in a teaspoon! They crawl into a pouch on their mother's stomach and stay there until they are about 10 weeks old. Then the young opossums ride around on their mother's back.

An opossum's tail is long and strong. The opossum uses it to hang from trees and prop itself up when it sits and eats roots, insects, fruit, and small animals. It can even carry things with its tail!

15 How long do baby opossums stay in their mother's pouch?

- ○ for 20 days
- ○ until they are 10 weeks old
- ○ until they are 20 weeks old
- ○ until they are a year old

16 What part of its body does an opossum use to hang from trees?

- ○ its front paws
- ○ its rear paws
- ○ its strong jaws
- ○ its tail

Birds are warm-blooded animals. They are able to control their body temperature, regardless of the outside weather. Their hearts beat very rapidly, using a great deal of energy. In order to maintain this energy, most birds must eat several times an hour. Some baby birds eat their own weight in food a day.

17 What is true about a bird's heart?

- ○ It does not pump blood.
- ○ It weighs as much as a baby bird.
- ○ It has feathers.
- ○ It beats very quickly.

14 Why must birds eat several times each hour?

- ○ to control the weather
- ○ to stay in practice
- ○ to keep up their energy
- ○ to gain weight when they are older

Answers: 15 until they are 10 weeks old; **16** its tail; **17** It beats very quickly. **18** to keep up their energy

GO ON

Once upon a time, there were two cousins, a town mouse and a country mouse. The town mouse was rich, and lived an exciting life in the city.

His cousin, who was very poor, lived a quiet life in the country. He had a small house near the edge of an empty field. It was not much to look at, but it was safely hidden away under a hedge.

One day, the country mouse invited the town mouse to come for a visit. He had stored up some nuts and grains of wheat, a few dried beans and peas, and some old crusts of bread. There were even a few scraps of cheese tucked away in the cupboard.

When the town mouse arrived, the country mouse did his best to make him feel comfortable and right at home. He brought out dish after dish of plain but tasty food, and set it before his well-bred cousin. The town mouse was not very impressed with the meal, but he did not want to hurt his host's feelings. So he nibbled a bit here, and picked a bit there, just to be polite.

After dinner, they sat around and talked. But before long, the town mouse began to long for some excitement. Finally, he could not stand the quiet any longer.

"But it is true," replied the town mouse. "Here in the country, one boring day just leads to the next. You can't afford to let life pass you by! After all, a mouse does not live forever. So why not come to town with me? Let me show you what it's like to really live!"

And so the country mouse agreed to go into town with his cousin. "You won't be sorry," said the town mouse. "In fact, you'll like it so much that you'll never come back to the country." Then they set out across the field, and left the quiet countryside behind.

19 What did the town mouse want the country mouse to do?

- ○ learn to cook better
- ○ learn to play the piano
- ○ stop hunting for food
- ○ move to town

20 Which word does the writer use to describe the town mouse's life in town?

- ○ wet
- ○ dangerous
- ○ safe
- ○ exciting

21 What does the town mouse think about country life?

- ○ It is safe.
- ○ It is full of tasty food.
- ○ It is boring.
- ○ It is exciting but in a different way.

22 What kind of food does not impress the town mouse?

- ○ plain food
- ○ fancy food
- ○ food he makes himself
- ○ only cheese

23 What does the town mouse promise to do for the country mouse?

- ○ teach him to cook
- ○ make him never want to go back to the country
- ○ keep him safe from hawks
- ○ lend him money

24 What does the town mouse do so he doesn't hurt his cousin's feelings?

- ○ He complains about everything.
- ○ He says how much he likes country life.
- ○ He wears old clothes.
- ○ He eats some of the food.

25 Why couldn't the town mouse stand the quiet any longer?

- ○ He was used to more excitement.
- ○ A letter asked him to go back home.
- ○ He wanted to make the country mouse feel bad.
- ○ He did not want to eat more cheese.

26 Which reason probably convinces the country mouse to go to town?

- ○ Food is better there.
- ○ Don't let life pass you by.
- ○ You will meet all my friends.
- ○ You will be rich.

STOP

Answers: 19 move to town; **20** exciting; **21** It is boring; **22** plain food; **23** make him never want to go back to the country; **24** He eats some of the food; **25** He was used to more excitement; **26** Don't let life pass you by.

Read Aloud

In this part of the test, you will decide what could not happen in real life.

Put your finger on Sample C.

Read the answer choices carefully. Then darken the circle next to the sentence that tells something that could not happen.

Give students time to do Sample C on their own. Then explain that sandboxes can't scream because they are not alive. The other three sentences tell about real things that could happen.

Now put your finger on number 27. Do numbers 27 to 30 in the same way we did Sample C.

Work until you reach the stop sign at the bottom of the page. Then put your pencils down.

Begin now.

Answers: C The sandbox screamed. **27** The milk poured itself into a glass. **28** Linda gave the ladder a sweater because it was cold. **29** Fish walked across the floor. **30** Tim's family went to Mars for the weekend.

Sample C

- ○ The playground was full of children.
- ○ Babies played in the sandbox.
- ○ The sandbox screamed.
- ○ Older children played on the swings.

27
- ○ Tom made a sandwich.
- ○ He washed the knife.
- ○ The milk poured itself into a glass.
- ○ Tom dropped his sandwich on the floor.

28
- ○ Alice swept the stairs.
- ○ Joey took out the trash.
- ○ Mandy washed the windows.
- ○ Linda gave the ladder a sweater because it was cold.

29
- ○ The pet shop owner said hello.
- ○ The store sells food for every kind of pet.
- ○ Rabbits hopped in a pen.
- ○ Fish walked across the floor.

30
- ○ Tim's family went to Mars for the weekend.
- ○ My family stays at home.
- ○ My cousins and I played soccer.
- ○ I scored the only goal.

STOP

Spelling Learn and Practice Strategies for Success

13. Finding the Word That Is Spelled Correctly

Plan

Remember to put the directions in your own words.

Glance at the answer choices. Guess what the word is. Spell it to yourself first. Then look for your spelling in the choices.

I won't let myself get confused. I know the right spelling.

Do

Darken the circle next to the word that is spelled correctly.

Sample A

I left my _____ in school.

○ cote
○ kote
○ coat
○ koat

STOP

1 The flower's leaves are _____.

○ purple
○ purpul
○ purpull
○ purpol

2 Sally will _____ me to skate.

○ teech
○ teche
○ teach
○ teeche

3 The person who took my cap is a _____.

○ thef
○ theef
○ thief
○ theif

4 I broke a _____ bowl.

○ glas
○ glaz
○ glase
○ glass

5 The closet door is _____.

○ lockt
○ loked
○ lokd
○ locked

6 The rain made the _____ wet.

○ earth
○ eorth
○ erth
○ erthe

STOP

Answers: A coat; **1** purple; **2** teach; **3** thief; **4** glass; **5** locked; **6** earth

14. Finding the Word That Is <u>Not</u> Spelled Correctly

Plan

Put the directions in your own words. What <u>two</u> things do they tell you to do?

Say each word to yourself. Eliminate words you know are spelled right.

If only one word is wrong, then the other words are correct. I'll look for the wrong word.

Do

Darken the circle next to the word that is <u>not</u> spelled correctly. If there are <u>no</u> spelling errors, darken the circle next to *No Mistakes*.

Sample A

- ○ computer
- ○ zero
- ○ botum
- ○ jump
- ○ *No Mistakes*

STOP

1
- ○ card
- ○ book
- ○ bocks
- ○ paper
- ○ *No Mistakes*

2
- ○ string
- ○ pants
- ○ coat
- ○ book
- ○ *No Mistakes*

3
- ○ dust
- ○ fish
- ○ sign
- ○ arro
- ○ *No Mistakes*

4
- ○ tear
- ○ boile
- ○ fix
- ○ sticks
- ○ *No Mistakes*

5
- ○ bright
- ○ fair
- ○ front
- ○ chilren
- ○ *No Mistakes*

6
- ○ miror
- ○ might
- ○ letter
- ○ cents
- ○ *No Mistakes*

STOP

Answers: A botum (bottom); **1** bocks (box); **2** No Mistakes; **3** arro (arrow); **4** boile (boil); **5** chilren (children); **6** miror (mirror)

Spelling

Time (optional): 20 minutes

Read Aloud

In this part of the test, you will pick words that are spelled correctly.

Put your finger on Sample A.

Read the sentence and the answer choices carefully. Then darken the circle next to the word that is spelled correctly.

Give students time to do Sample A on their own. Then explain that of the choices, only g-l-o-v-e-s *is spelled correctly.*

Now put your finger on number 1. Do numbers 1 to 6 in the same way we did Sample A.

Work until you reach the stop sign at the bottom of the page. Then put your pencils down.

Begin now.

Answers: A gloves; **1** wheat; **2** greet; **3** Tuesday; **4** shoes; **5** February; **6** lazy

Sample A

Wear warm _____ today.

- ○ gluvs
- ○ gloves
- ○ glovs
- ○ gluvz

STOP

1 This bread is _____ bread.

- ○ whete
- ○ wheat
- ○ weet
- ○ wheet

2 Stand up and _____ our guest.

- ○ greete
- ○ greate
- ○ grete
- ○ greet

3 On _____ we will go skating.

- ○ Toosday
- ○ Tusday
- ○ Tuesday
- ○ Touesday

4 Where are your _____?

- ○ shoes
- ○ shuze
- ○ shuz
- ○ shooz

5 Our vacation is in _____.

- ○ Febuary
- ○ February
- ○ Feberry
- ○ Februeary

6 The _____ dog slept all day.

- ○ lazey
- ○ lasy
- ○ lazee
- ○ lazy

STOP

Read Aloud

In this part of the test, you will pick words that are not spelled correctly.

Put your finger on Sample B.

Read the answer choices carefully. Then darken the circle next to the word that is not spelled correctly. If there are no spelling errors, darken the circle next to *No Mistakes.*

Give students time to do Sample B on their own. Then explain that friend *is spelled* f-r-i-e-n-d. *The other words are spelled correctly.*

Now put your finger on number 7. Do numbers 7 to 12 in the same way we did Sample B.

Work until you reach the stop sign at the bottom of the page. Then put your pencils down.

Begin now.

Answers: B frend; **7** bottel (bottle); **8** everyun (everyone); **9** ribun (ribbon); **10** kan't (can't); **11** No Mistakes; **12** stor (store)

Sample B

- ○ bow
- ○ brain
- ○ frend
- ○ foot
- ○ *No Mistakes*

7
- ○ bottel
- ○ break
- ○ farm
- ○ toys
- ○ No Mistakes

8
- ○ everyun
- ○ light
- ○ thick
- ○ fan
- ○ *No Mistakes*

9
- ○ their
- ○ flowers
- ○ tape
- ○ ribun
- ○ *No Mistakes*

10
- ○ music
- ○ puzzle
- ○ November
- ○ kan't
- ○ *No Mistakes*

11
- ○ storm
- ○ fight
- ○ sorry
- ○ pain
- ○ *No Mistakes*

12
- ○ panda
- ○ punch
- ○ strong
- ○ stor
- ○ *No Mistakes*

Test 5

Language Mechanics

Learn and Practice Strategies for Success

15. Using Capital Letters Correctly

Plan

Tell yourself what you need to do. Put the directions in your own words.

Read the entire sentence. Then decide where <u>you</u> think a capital letter is needed. Look for your answer in the choices.

See how the format is different. The lines divide the sentence into three parts. Make sure you mark the circle under the right part.

We use capital letters for proper names. They're the real names of people, places, and things.

Do

Darken the circle under the part of the sentence that needs a capital letter. Darken the circle for *None* if <u>no</u> capital letter is needed.

Sample A

The lost airplane ○ | finally landed ○ | in boston. ○ | ○ *None*

STOP

1 The golden gate bridge ○ | in California ○ | is very long. ○ | ○ *None*

2 My friend jeff ○ | won first prize ○ | in the contest. ○ | ○ *None*

3 Who wrote ○ | the book ○ | named <u>milk truck</u>? ○ | ○ *None*

4 Rosa and ○ | tom are ○ | neighbors now. ○ | ○ *None*

5 We go ○ | to the beach often ○ | in july. ○ | ○ *None*

STOP

Answers: A in boston (Boston); **1** The golden gate bridge (Golden Gate Bridge); **2** My friend jeff (Jeff); **3** named <u>milk truck</u> (<u>Milk Truck</u>); **4** tom are (Tom); **5** in july (July)

16. Using Punctuation Correctly

Plan

Tell yourself what you need to do. Put the directions in your own words.

Read the entire sentence. Then decide where <u>you</u> would add a punctuation mark and which one you need. Look for your answer in the choices.

I decide to use a (.), a (?), or an (!) depending on what the sentence means.

Answers: A question mark; **1** period; **2** period; **3** exclamation mark; **4** None; **5** question mark

Do

Darken the circle next to the punctuation mark that would make the sentence correct. Darken the circle for *None* if <u>no</u> other punctuation is needed.

Sample A

Is this seat empty

○ .　　○ ?　　○ !　　○ *None*

---

1 Please help your brother with the game

○ .　　○ ?　　○ !　　○ *None*

2 The dog and the cat are on the porch

○ .　　○ ?　　○ !　　○ *None*

3 What a hot day today is

○ .　　○ ?　　○ !　　○ *None*

4 Will we see fireworks this July?

○ .　　○ ?　　○ !　　○ *None*

5 Where did you leave the mop, Tim

○ .　　○ ?　　○ !　　○ *None*

17. Using Capital Letters and Punctuation in Writing

Plan

Tell yourself what you need to do. Put the directions in your own words.

Read the entire sentence or paragraph. Then decide how <u>you</u> would fix the mistakes you find. Look for your correction in the choices.

See how the format is different.

- The numbers in ( ) tell you the part of the sentence the question is about.
- Make sure to match up the number with the right words.

I won't let myself get confused. First I'll read each answer choice. I'll tell myself how it's different from the one before. Then I'll see if it's the correction I wanted to make.

Answers: **A** no milk. The carton; **1** day it is! Soccer; **2** dressed. They put; **3** coaches. The coaches; **4** team will win

Do

Darken the circle next to the choice that shows the correct capitalization and punctuation for the underlined part. Darken the circle for *Correct as it is* if there is <u>no</u> error.

Sample A

We have <u>no milk. the carton</u> is empty.

- ○ no milk the carton
- ○ no milk The carton
- ○ no milk. The carton
- ○ *Correct as it is*

(1) What an exciting <u>day it is? Soccer</u> season starts
in an hour. The players on both teams are getting
(2) <u>dressed. they put</u> on their shin guards. They put on
(3) their cleats. They listen to their <u>coaches the coaches</u>
give them final instructions. Then they are ready to
(4) play. The players hope their <u>team will. win.</u>

1
- ○ day it is! Soccer
- ○ day it is soccer
- ○ Day it is! soccer
- ○ *Correct as it is*

2
- ○ dressed they put
- ○ dressed? They put
- ○ dressed. They put
- ○ *Correct as it is*

3
- ○ Coaches. the coaches
- ○ coaches. The coaches
- ○ coaches? the coaches
- ○ *Correct as it is*

4
- ○ team will win.
- ○ Team will win.
- ○ team. will. win.
- ○ *Correct as it is*

I'll really pay attention when I read.

(5) <u>may 1 1998</u>

(6) <u>Dear Aunt rnary</u>

(7) Thank you for the <u>birthday gift. i</u> needed more gravel for my fish tank. Now I have enough for a long time to come.

(8) <u>sincerely</u>
Brenda

5 ○ May 1, 1998,
○ May 1, 1998
○ May, 1, 1998
○ *Correct as it is*

7 ○ Birthday gift. I
○ birthday gift. I
○ birthday gift I
○ *Correct as it is*

6 ○ dear Aunt Mary,
○ Dear: Aunt Mary
○ Dear Aunt Mary,
○ *Correct as it is*

8 ○ Sincerely,
○ Sincerely
○ Sincerely.
○ *Correct as it is*

(9) <u>We cant cross</u> the street safely. There have been
(10) four big accidents at that <u>corner The town</u> needs a traffic light there.

9 ○ We can't. Cross
○ We. Can't cross
○ We can't cross
○ *Correct as it is*

10 ○ corner. The town
○ corner? The town
○ corner the town
○ *Correct as it is*

Answers: 5 May 1, 1998 **6** Dear Aunt Mary,; **7** birthday gift. I; **8** Sincerely,; **9** We can't cross; **10** corner. The town

Language Mechanics

Time (optional): 15 minutes

Read Aloud
In this part of the test, you will decide if capital letters are used correctly.

Put your finger on Sample A.

Read the sentence carefully. Darken the circle under the part of the sentence that needs a capital letter. Darken the circle for *None* if no capital letter is needed.

Give students time to do Sample A on their own. Then explain that December is the name of a month, and the names of months should start with capital letters.

Now put your finger on number 1. Do numbers 1 to 6 in the same way we did Sample A.

Work until you reach the stop sign at the bottom of the page. Then put your pencils down.

Begin now.

Answers: A in december (December); **1** his son kevin (Kevin); **2** is helena (Helena); **3** named intrepid (Intrepid); **4** Thomas edison (Edison); **5** in Los angeles (Angeles); **6** Mother and ellen (Ellen)

Sample A

Winter starts | in december | every year.
○ ○ ○ ○ *None*

STOP

1 Dan called to | his son kevin | in the yard.
○ ○ ○ ○ *None*

2 The capital | of Montana | is helena.
○ ○ ○ ○ *None*

3 A warship | named intrepid | is now a museum.
○ ○ ○ ○ *None*

4 Thomas edison | invented | the lightbulb.
○ ○ ○ ○ *None*

5 This movie | was made | in Los angeles.
○ ○ ○ ○ *None*

6 Mother and ellen | went shopping | for food.
○ ○ ○ ○ *None*

Read Aloud

In this part of the test, you will decide if punctuation marks are used correctly.

Put your finger on Sample B.

Read the sentence carefully. Darken the circle next to the punctuation mark that would make the sentence correct. Darken the circle for *None* if no other punctuation is needed.

Give students time to do Sample B on their own. Then explain that the sentence is a telling sentence, and telling sentences end with a period.

Now put your finger on number 7. Do numbers 7 to 12 in the same way we did Sample A.

Work until you reach the stop sign at the bottom of the page. Then put your pencils down.

Begin now.

Answers: B period; **7** question mark; **8** exclamation mark; **9** period; **10** question mark; **11** question mark; **12** period

Sample B

We brought sleeping bags to camp

O .   O ?   O !   O *None*

STOP

7 Where are the wild animals

O .   O ?   O !   O *None*

8 What a giant puddle the rain left

O .   O ?   O !   O *None*

9 I like oranges better than grapes

O .   O ?   O !   O *None*

10 Who left the cat food in the car

O .   O ?   O !   O *None*

11 Why don't you ask a question

O .   O ?   O !   O *None*

12 Emmet can't find his cap

O .   O ?   O !   O *None*

Read Aloud

In this part of the test, you will decide if capital letters and punctuation marks are used correctly.

Put your finger on Sample C.

Read the sentence and the answer choices carefully. Darken the circle next to the choice that shows the correct capitalization and punctuation for the underlined part. Darken the circle for *Correct as it is* if there is no error.

Give students time to do Sample C on their own. Then explain that Recess is over *and* Everyone is going inside *are two separate telling sentences. Therefore,* Recess is over *must end with a period.*

Now put your finger on number 13. Do numbers 13 to 24 in the same way we did Sample C.

Work until you reach the stop sign at the bottom of the next page. Then put your pencils down.

Begin now.

Answers: C over. Everyone; **13** White House. That's; **14** lives. We hoped; **15** Correct as it is; **16** Dear Uncle Marty,; **17** tree. Thank you; **18** Yours truly,

Sample C

Recess is over Everyone is going inside.

- ○ over everyone
- ○ over. Everyone
- ○ over? Everyone
- ○ *Correct as it is*

STOP

---

(13) We visited the white house. That's where
(14) the President lives we hoped we would see him.

13
- ○ White House. That's
- ○ White house. That's
- ○ White House. Thats
- ○ *Correct as it is*

14
- ○ lives? We hoped
- ○ Lives. We hoped
- ○ lives. We hoped
- ○ *Correct as it is*

(15) October 5, 1998
(16) Dear Uncle marty
(17) The wind blew my old kite into a tree. thank you for buying me a new one. Maybe we can fly it together.
(18) yours truly
Bobby

15
- ○ october 5 1998
- ○ October 5 1998
- ○ October 5, 1998,
- ○ *Correct as it is*

17
- ○ tree thank you
- ○ Tree. Thank you
- ○ tree. Thank you
- ○ *Correct as it is*

16
- ○ Dear Uncle Marty,
- ○ Dear Uncle marty,
- ○ Dear Uncle, Marty
- ○ *Correct as it is*

18
- ○ Yours truly,
- ○ yours, truly
- ○ yours, Truly
- ○ *Correct as it is*

GO ON

(19) Everyone has a project to do. my project is about
(20) Liberia That's a country in Africa. Monrovia is the capital of Liberia. The city is named for James
(21) monroe. He was the fifth president of the United
(22) states? Freed slaves from our country founded Liberia in 1822.

19
- ○ to do my project
- ○ to do my project.
- ○ to do. My project
- ○ *Correct as it is*

21
- ○ monroe he
- ○ Monroe. he
- ○ Monroe. He
- ○ *Correct as it is*

20
- ○ Liberia that's
- ○ Liberia. That's
- ○ Liberia. Thats
- ○ *Correct as it is*

22
- ○ States. Freed
- ○ States freed
- ○ States freed.
- ○ *Correct as it is*

(23) My cousin's school gives music lessons I want
(24) to learn the piano. my cousin is learning the violin.

23
- ○ lessons. I want
- ○ Lessons. I want
- ○ lessons? I want
- ○ *Correct as it is*

24
- ○ Piano my cousin.
- ○ piano. my Cousin
- ○ piano. My cousin
- ○ *Correct as it is*

Answers: 19 to do. My project; **20** Liberia. That's; **21** Monroe. He; **22** States. Freed; **23** lessons. I want; **24** piano. My cousin

Test 6

Language Usage

Learn and Practice Strategies for Success

18. Choosing Correct Usage

Plan

Tell yourself what you need to do. Put the directions in your own words.

Notice the change in format. Read the entire test item first. Then go back and look for the mistake. Think about how you would write the sentence.

Fill in only one circle for each number. Erase your old answer completely if you change your mind.

I'll say each line to myself. I'll look for words that don't sound right to me.

Answers: A The two boys walks to school together (walk); **1** but not whens I use (when); **2** but he don't got enough paint (doesn't have); **3** They ain't saying (aren't); **4** cross the street by hisself (himself)

Do

Darken the circle next to the line that has a mistake in the way words are used. Darken the circle for No mistakes if there are no mistakes.

Sample A

- ○ The two boys walks to school together
- ○ because they are good friends
- ○ and they live near each other.
- ○ *No mistakes*

1
- ○ I can tell time on a digital watch,
- ○ but not whens I use
- ○ a clock with hands.
- ○ *No mistakes*

2
- ○ He wants to paint the bike,
- ○ but he don't got enough paint
- ○ for the whole job.
- ○ *No mistakes*

3
- ○ They ain't saying
- ○ when they plan
- ○ to let us play basketball with them.
- ○ *No mistakes*

4
- ○ My Mom and Dad let my brother
- ○ cross the street by hisself,
- ○ but they won't let me.
- ○ *No mistakes*

GO ON

How would a writer say this in a book?

5 ○ On Saturday Sue and me
○ went to the new mall
○ to buy a gift for Mom.
○ *No mistakes*

6 ○ The girls made snacks
○ and bringed them next door
○ for their friends.
○ *No mistakes*

7 ○ They coats were wet
○ when they came indoors
○ during the big storm.
○ No mistakes

I'll need to keep paying attention. I can't let my mind wander.

8 ○ My big sister
○ found the holders
○ for the birthday candles.
○ *No mistakes*

9 ○ Libby breaked a dish
○ and threw the pieces
○ into the trash can.
○ *No mistakes*

10 ○ Jake's shirt was dirty,
○ so he put on the same shirt
○ that he wored yesterday.
○ *No mistakes*

STOP

Answers: 5 On Saturday Sue and me (I); **6** and bringed them next door (brought); **7** They coats were wet (Their); **8** No mistakes; **9** Libby breaked a dish (broke); **10** that he wored yesterday (wore)

19. Finding Subjects

Plan

Tell yourself what you need to do. Put the directions in your own words.

The simple subject of a sentence is a naming word. It names the main person, place, idea, or thing that the sentence tells about.

To find the subject, look for an action word. The action word in Sample A is ran. Then ask yourself, who or what ran?

Make sure to darken the circle under the right word.

I'll remember to start with the action word.

PLANNING NOTE

Subtests 19–21 (Finding Subjects, Finding Predicates, and Analyzing Paragraphs) are appropriate mainly for third grade students. If you teach students below grade 3, you may wish to skip pages 59–62.

Answers: A horse; **1** birds; **2** apple; **3** eagle; **4** wind; **5** Broncos; **6** wind; **7** Rabbits

Do

Darken the circle under the simple subject of each sentence.

Sample A

The horse ran back to the stable.

○ ○ ○ ○

STOP

1 The birds found the bread on the ground.

○ ○ ○ ○

2 The apple has a soft spot on top.

○ ○ ○ ○

3 An eagle soared in the sky far above the earth.

○ ○ ○ ○

4 The wind pushed the sailboat across the lake.

○ ○ ○ ○

5 The Broncos beat my team in soccer.

○ ○ ○ ○

6 The wind slammed the door in my face.

○ ○ ○ ○

7 Rabbits ate all the carrots in the garden.

○ ○ ○ ○

STOP

20. Finding Predicates

Plan

Tell yourself what you need to do. Put the directions in your own words.

The simple predicate of a sentence is an action word. It tells what happened.

To find the simple predicate, picture the sentence in your mind. What action do you see happening? The word that names that action is the simple predicate.

Make sure to darken the circle under the right word.

Action words are "doing" words. What is someone or something doing?

Answers: A carried; **1** played; **2** heard; **3** stood; **4** saluted; **5** scored; **6** crossed; **7** waved

Do

Darken the circle under the simple predicate of each sentence.

Sample A

Freddy carried his dishes to the sink.

STOP

1 The dog played with a toy bone.

2 We heard the news about the fire.

3 The soldier stood with her hands at her sides.

4 The class saluted the flag on the wall.

5 Rosie scored the last goal of the game.

6 The runner crossed the busy street.

7 Hundreds of people at the party waved flags

21. Analyzing Paragraphs

Plan

Read for a purpose.

First read the questions that come after the paragraph. Read just the questions. Skip the answer choices.

Then read the paragraph. Keep those questions in mind as you read.

Next go back to the questions. Read all the answer choices. Pick the best one. Darken the circle next to it.

Notice the little numbers in the paragraph. They tell you the sentence number.

I'll really pay attention when I read.

Answers: A sentence 5 (off the topic); **1** Dogs can be more than just pets. (summary topic sentence); **2** sentence 5 (off the topic)

Do

Darken the circle next to the correct answer.

Sample A

[1]The runners stood still. [2]They waited for the race to start. [3]Some runners felt nervous. [4]Other runners couldn't wait to start. [5]The Olympics have races, too. [6]The coach shouted, "Go!" and off they ran.

Which sentence does <u>not</u> belong in this paragraph?

- ○ sentence 1
- ○ sentence 3
- ○ sentence 4
- ○ sentence 5

---

[1]Some dogs are guard dogs. [2]They protect people from harm. [3]Some dogs are rescue dogs. [4]They find people who are lost in the woods. [5]Pet birds don't do this. [6]They find people who are trapped in wrecked buildings. [7]Other dogs are work dogs. [8]They herd sheep and cattle. [9]They keep the farm running.

1 What is the best opening sentence for this paragraph?

- ○ Dogs and canaries are fun.
- ○ Here's how to take care of your pet dog.
- ○ Dogs can be more than just pets.
- ○ There are many breeds of dog.

2 Which sentence does not belong in this paragraph?

- ○ sentence 2
- ○ sentence 5
- ○ sentence 8
- ○ sentence 9

I'll remember to read the questions first. My purpose for reading is to find the answer to these questions.

Remember to keep your finger on the number of the question you are working on.

Don't forget. If you skip a question, come back to it.

[1]Snacks are nice. [2]The boys like chips. [3]The girls like apples and oranges more than chips. [4]We all agree that candy is a special treat. [5]We could get cavities. [6]Our families don't want us to eat too many sweets. [7]Candy can make us gain weight, too. [8]Is any fruit salty?

3 Where does sentence 5 belong?

- ○ before sentence 2
- ○ before sentence 3
- ○ before sentence 4
- ○ before sentence 7

4 Which is a better opening sentence than sentence 1?

- ○ Snacks are tasty.
- ○ Everyone has a favorite snack, but some snacks cause trouble.
- ○ I like snacks a lot.
- ○ Some snacks are even good for you.

5 Which sentence does not belong in this paragraph?

- ○ sentence 2
- ○ sentence 6
- ○ sentence 7
- ○ sentence 8

6 What is the best closing sentence for this paragraph?

- ○ Pineapple slices are tasty, too.
- ○ Kids deserve snacks.
- ○ Nice snacks are tasty.
- ○ Snacks should keep us healthy, not hurt us.

[1]I go with my Mom to the library every Saturday. [2]We look at the new books. [3]We look at the books people brought back. [4]Then we pick one we like. [5]I sit with my Mom in a big old chair they have there. [6]We read the book to each other. [7]I play sports, too. [8]Saturday is the best day of the week.

7 What is the best opening sentence for this paragraph?

- ○ The library is on Dix Road.
- ○ Saturday is the first day of the weekend.
- ○ Saturday is a special day for me.
- ○ Well, here's what I do.

8 Which sentence does not belong in this paragraph?

- ○ sentence 3
- ○ sentence 5
- ○ sentence 7
- ○ sentence 8

STOP

Answers: 3 before sentence 7; **4** Everyone has a favorite snack, but some snacks cause trouble; **5** sentence 8; **6** Snacks should keep us healthy, not hurt us; **7** Saturday is a special day for me; **8** sentence 7

Language Usage

Time (optional): 30 minutes

Read Aloud

In this part of the test, you will decide if there are mistakes in the way words are used.

Put your finger on Sample A.

Read the sentence carefully. Darken the circle next to the line that has a mistake in the way words are used. Darken the circle for *No mistakes* if there are no mistakes.

Give students time to do Sample A on their own. Then explain that line 2, because he don't know, *contains a mistake. In English we use* doesn't *with* he, she, *and* it. *We use* don't *with* I, you, we, *and* they.

Now put your finger on number 1. Do numbers 1 to 10 in the same way we did Sample A.

Work until you reach the stop sign at the bottom of the page. Then put your pencils down.

Begin now.

Answers: A because he don't know (doesn't); **1** The toys falled off the shelf (fell); **2** Me and my friends (My friends and I); **3** but we didn't see no clowns (any); **4** I leaved my hat on the bus (left)

Sample A

○ John will be late
○ because he don't know
○ what time it is.
○ *No mistakes*

1 ○ The toys falled off the shelf
○ when Lily hit it
○ with the shopping cart.
○ *No mistakes*

2 ○ Me and my friends
○ watched a hockey game
○ at the ice skating rink.
○ *No mistakes*

3 ○ We went to the circus,
○ but we didn't see no clowns
○ until the end of the show.
○ *No mistakes*

4 ○ I was sad
○ when I discovered
○ I leaved my hat on the bus.
○ *No mistakes*

GO ON

5 ○ We wanted
○ to see a movie,
○ but we is staying home.
○ *No mistakes*

---

6 ○ I ain't surprised
○ that our soccer team
○ won the big game.
○ *No mistakes*

---

7 ○ During the game
○ no one found the clue
○ that we putted under the sofa.
○ *No mistakes*

---

8 ○ This new space movie
○ is the worst movie
○ I have ever seed.
○ *No mistakes*

---

9 ○ My cousin Norma
○ is the bestest player
○ on her whole team.
○ *No mistakes*

---

10 ○ Nat didn't go swimming,
○ because he had a cold
○ and didn't feel well.
○ *No mistakes*

Answers: 5 but we is staying home (are); **6** I ain't surprised (am not); **7** that we putted under the sofa (put); **8** I have ever seed (seen); **9** is the bestest player (best); **10** No mistakes

PLANNING NOTE

If you omitted Subtests 19–21 (Finding Subjects, Finding Predicates, and Analyzing Paragraphs) on pages 59–62, have students also omit items 11–36 on pages 65–68 in the Timed Practice Test.

Read Aloud

In this part of the test, you will decide which word is the simple subject of a sentence.

Put your finger on Sample B.

Read the sentence carefully. Darken the circle under the word that is the simple subject of the sentence.

Give students time to do Sample B on their own. Then explain that the action word in the sentence is stood. *The word* people *answers the question, "who or what stood?"*

Now put your finger on number 11. Do numbers 11 to 18 in the same way we did Sample B.

Work until you reach the stop sign at the bottom of the page. Then put your pencils down.

Begin now.

Answers: B People; **11** Trucks; **12** cars; **13** Jess; **14** Angela; **15** cousins; **16** teacher; **17** aunt; **18** mother

Sample B

People stood on line for movie tickets.

STOP

11 Trucks delivered large piles of bricks.

12 The cars honked their horns loudly.

13 Jess read a book about spiders.

14 Angela enjoys books about ponies.

15 My cousins collect rocks and shells.

16 My teacher writes notes on our papers.

17 My aunt sent me a birthday card.

18 Joe's mother bought pizza for us.

Read Aloud

In this part of the test, you will decide which word is the simple predicate of a sentence.

Put your finger on Sample C.

Read the sentence carefully. Darken the circle under the simple predicate of the sentence.

Give students time to do Sample C on their own. Then explain that the "doing word" in Sample C is flew. Flew *tells what happened in the sentence.*

Now put your finger on number 19. Do numbers 19 to 26 in the same way we did Sample C.

Work until you reach the stop sign at the bottom of the page. Then put your pencils down.

Begin now.

Answers: C flew; **19** milked; **20** visit; **21** fixed; **22** roared; **23** stopped; **24** answered; **25** sold; **26** forgot

Sample C

The children flew kites in the park.

○ ○ ○ ○

STOP

19 The young girl milked the cows in the barn.

○ ○ ○ ○

20 Many people from town visit this park.

○ ○ ○ ○

21 The workers fixed the stairs quickly.

○ ○ ○ ○

22 The train suddenly roared into the station.

○ ○ ○ ○

23 The bus stopped in front of the door.

○ ○ ○ ○

24 Ralph answered the question correctly.

○ ○ ○ ○

25 We sold every ounce of lemonade.

○ ○ ○ ○

26 Mom and I forgot the doctor's address.

○ ○ ○ ○

Read Aloud

In this part of the test, you will analyze paragraphs and decide how to improve them.

Put your finger on Sample D.

Read the paragraph and the answer choices carefully. Darken the circle next to the correct answer.

Give students time to do Sample D on their own. Then explain that sentence 5 is off the topic and does not belong in the paragraph. It starts a new topic. It does not develop the topic begun in sentence 1.

Now put your finger on number 27. Do numbers 27 to 36 in the same way we did Sample D.

Work until you reach the stop sign at the bottom of the next page. Then put your pencils down.

Begin now.

Answers: C sentence **5** (off the topic); **27** A small airport is an exciting place to visit; **28** before sentence 3; **29** In minutes the plane was just a dot in the sky; **30** sentence 7

Sample D

[1]The school has a new playground. [2]Every class helped plan it. [3]The parents helped build it. [4]We're proud of what we did. [5]I'm also proud of other things. [6]Other schools can build playgrounds for themselves, too.

Which sentence does <u>not</u> belong in this paragraph?

- ○ sentence 1
- ○ sentence 3
- ○ sentence 5
- ○ sentence 6

STOP

---

[1]It was fun. [2]We saw a large plane. [3]It was getting ready for take-off. [4]Workers loaded suitcases into the hold. [5]It had two jet engines. [6]Then people walked out to board the plane. [7]It took us an hour to drive to the airport. [8]We stayed until we saw the airplane taxi to the end of the runway and take off.

27 Which is a better opening sentence than sentence 1?

- ○ I like airports.
- ○ Do you like to visit new places?
- ○ A small airport is an exciting place to visit.
- ○ We visited on Saturday.

28 Where does sentence 5 belong?

- ○ before sentence 1
- ○ before sentence 2
- ○ before sentence 3
- ○ before sentence 8

29 Which is the best closing sentence to add to this paragraph?

- ○ And that's the end of my story.
- ○ I hope you liked my story.
- ○ In minutes the plane was just a dot in the sky.
- ○ Yes, it was fun.

30 Which sentence does not belong in this paragraph?

- ○ sentence 3
- ○ sentence 4
- ○ sentence 7
- ○ sentence 8

[1]My family visited a farm. [2]We saw sheep, chickens and cows. [3]I liked the cows the most. [4]The farmer let us milk a cow by hand. [5]So the farmer showed us how the milking machine works. [6]My family once visited a cheese factory. [7]Hand-milking all 60 cows would be a big job. [8]We learned a lot.

31 Which is a better opening sentence than sentence 1?

- ○ Sunny Farms is nice.
- ○ Sunny Farms is a great place to spend a day.
- ○ We visited the farm.
- ○ Have you visited a farm?

32 Where does sentence 7 belong?

- ○ before sentence 2
- ○ before sentence 3
- ○ before sentence 4
- ○ before sentence 5

33 Which is ta better closing sentence than sentence 8?

- ○ We learned about farms.
- ○ We had a good time.
- ○ We learned firsthand that farming is hard work.
- ○ We left and drove home.

34 Which sentence does not belong in this paragraph?

- ○ sentence 3
- ○ sentence 4
- ○ sentence 5
- ○ sentence 6

[1]I had a sleep-over. [2]I stayed overnight at Jonah's house. [3]Jonah has two cats. [4]He also has two new computer games. [5]He has been my best friend ever since we were three years old. [6]I enjoyed playing the computer games and staying up late. [6]But it felt strange without my family there.

35 Which is a better opening sentence for this paragraph?

- ○ Saturday was my first sleep-over ever.
- ○ I have a sleeping bag.
- ○ We stayed up until 10:30 at night.
- ○ It was fun.

36 Where does sentence 5 belong?

- ○ before sentence 1
- ○ before sentence 2
- ○ before sentence 3
- ○ before sentence 4

STOP

Answers: 31 Sunny Farms is a great place to spend a day; **32** before sentence 5; **33** We learned firsthand that farming is hard work; **34** sentence 6; **35** Saturday was my first sleep-over ever; **36** before sentence 3

Test 7

Mathmatical Computation

Learn and Practice Strategies for Success

22. Adding Numbers

Plan

Remember if you must add or subtract the numbers.

Solve the problem yourself first. Then look for your answer in the choices.

Be sure to darken the circle for the answer you picked.

I can't find my answer. I'll add the numbers again.

To the Teacher *Please see the Planning Notes on pages 71 and 74.*

Scratch Paper If you wish, give students practice in using scratch paper. Tell them to use the scratch paper to find their answers.

Answers: A 6; **1** 11; **2** 25; **3** 79; **4** 62; **5** 450; **6** 429

Do

Darken the circle next to the correct answer.

Sample A
Add

$$\begin{array}{r} 4 \\ +2 \\ \hline \end{array}$$

○ 4
○ 5
○ 6
○ 7

STOP

1

6 + 5 =

○ 1
○ 10
○ 11
○ 12

2

$$\begin{array}{r} 10 \\ +15 \\ \hline \end{array}$$

○ 5
○ 12
○ 15
○ 25

3

$$\begin{array}{r} 42 \\ +37 \\ \hline \end{array}$$

○ 75
○ 77
○ 79
○ 80

4

$$\begin{array}{r} 54 \\ +\ 8 \\ \hline \end{array}$$

○ 52
○ 61
○ 62
○ 64

5

$$\begin{array}{r} 300 \\ +150 \\ \hline \end{array}$$

○ 400
○ 450
○ 500
○ 600

6

$$\begin{array}{r} 173 \\ +256 \\ \hline \end{array}$$

○ 323
○ 423
○ 429
○ 539

STOP

23. Subtracting Numbers

Plan

Remember if you must add or subtract the numbers.

Solve the problem yourself first. Then look for your answer in the choices.

Check your answer. Add your answer to the second number. You should get the first number.

Darken only one answer circle for each problem.

I won't lose my place. I'll darken the right circle.

Scratch Paper If you wish, give students practice in using scratch paper. Tell them to use the scratch paper to find their answers.

Answers: A 5; **1** 6; **2** 9; **3** 32; **4** 19; **5** 333; **6** 79

Do

Darken the circle next to the correct answer.

Sample A
Subtract

8 – 3 =

- ○ 3
- ○ 5
- ○ 8
- ○ 11

STOP

1

$$\begin{array}{r} 13 \\ \underline{-\ 7} \end{array}$$

- ○ 6
- ○ 8
- ○ 10
- ○ 20

2

17 - 8 =

- ○ 7
- ○ 9
- ○ 11
- ○ 25

3

$$\begin{array}{r} 45 \\ \underline{-\ 13} \end{array}$$

- ○ 13
- ○ 22
- ○ 28
- ○ 32

4

$$\begin{array}{r} 76 \\ \underline{-\ 57} \end{array}$$

- ○ 11
- ○ 21
- ○ 19
- ○ 29

5

$$\begin{array}{r} 395 \\ \underline{-\ 62} \end{array}$$

- ○ 235
- ○ 237
- ○ 333
- ○ 337

6

$$\begin{array}{r} 247 \\ \underline{-\ 168} \end{array}$$

- ○ 65
- ○ 75
- ○ 79
- ○ 115

24. Multiplying and Dividing Numbers

Plan

Read the problem. Which sign do you find: X (for multiply) or ÷ (for divide)? What other sign means to divide?

Remember which sign the problem has.

Solve the problem yourself first.
Then look for your answer in the choices.

Check your answers to division problems. Multiply your answer by the number you divided by. The result should be the other number.

Be sure to darken the circle for the answer you picked.

If you can't do a problem, skip it.
Come back to it later.

I can't find my answer. I'll divide the numbers again.

PLANNING NOTE

Subtest 24, Multiplying and Dividing Numbers, is appropriate mainly for third grade students. If you teach students below grade 3, you may wish to skip page 71.

Scratch Paper If you wish, give students practice in using scratch paper. Tell them to use the scratch paper to find their answers.

Answers: A 14; **B** 4; **1** 56; **2** 6; **3** 1500; **4** 9; **5** 156; **6** 70

Do

Darken the circle next to the correct answer.

Sample A
Multiply

7 X 2 =

- ○ 9
- ○ 12
- ○ 14
- ○ 16

Sample B
Divide

12 ÷ 3 =

- ○ 3
- ○ 4
- ○ 5
- ○ 6

STOP

1

8 X 7 =

- ○ 48
- ○ 56
- ○ 64
- ○ 72

2

36 ÷ 6 =

- ○ 4
- ○ 6
- ○ 8
- ○ 12

3

$$\begin{array}{r} 75 \\ \underline{\times\ 20} \end{array}$$

- ○ 150
- ○ 300
- ○ 1500
- ○ 15000

4

81 ÷ 9 =

- ○ 3
- ○ 5
- ○ 7
- ○ 9

5

$$\begin{array}{r} 13 \\ \underline{\times\ 12} \end{array}$$

- ○ 25
- ○ 136
- ○ 144
- ○ 156

6

$3\overline{)210}$

- ○ 7
- ○ 10
- ○ 21
- ○ 70

STOP

Mathematical Computation

Time (optional): 20 minutes

Read Aloud
In this part of the test, you will add two numbers.

Put your finger on Sample A.

Read the numbers and the answer choices carefully. Then darken the circle next to the correct answer.

Give students time to do Sample A on their own. Then explain that 4 plus 3 equals 7.

Now put your finger on number 1. Do numbers 1 to 6 in the same way we did Sample A.

Work until you reach the stop sign at the bottom of the page. Then put your pencils down.

Begin now.

To the Teacher *Please see the Planning Note on page 74.*

Scratch Paper If you wish, give students practice in using scratch paper. Tell them to use the scratch paper to find their answers.

Answers: A 7; **1** 8; **2** 18; **3** 29; **4** 69; **5** 100; **6** 692

Sample A
Add

4 + 3 =

- ○ 0
- ○ 7
- ○ 8
- ○ 70

1

$$\begin{array}{r} 3 \\ +\ 5 \\ \hline \end{array}$$

- ○ 7
- ○ 7
- ○ 8
- ○ 10

2

4 + 14 =

- ○ 6
- ○ 14
- ○ 18
- ○ 20

3

$$\begin{array}{r} 16 \\ +\ 13 \\ \hline \end{array}$$

- ○ 25
- ○ 28
- ○ 29
- ○ 30

4

$$\begin{array}{r} 44 \\ +\ 25 \\ \hline \end{array}$$

- ○ 55
- ○ 59
- ○ 69
- ○ 71

5

$$\begin{array}{r} 63 \\ +\ 37 \\ \hline \end{array}$$

- ○ 90
- ○ 91
- ○ 94
- ○ 100

6

$$\begin{array}{r} 283 \\ +\ 409 \\ \hline \end{array}$$

- ○ 582
- ○ 692
- ○ 702
- ○ 712

STOP

Read Aloud
In this part of the test, you will subtract two numbers.

Put your finger on Sample B.

Read the numbers and the answer choices carefully. Then darken the circle next to the correct answer.

Give students time to do Sample B on their own. Then explain that 11 minus 4 is 7.

Now put your finger on number 7. Do numbers 7 to 12 in the same way we did Sample B.

Work until you reach the stop sign at the bottom of the page. Then put your pencils down.

Begin now.

Scratch Paper If you wish, give students practice in using scratch paper. Tell them to use the scratch paper to find their answers.

Answers: B 7; **7** 13; **8** 2; **9** 2; **10** 25; **11** 129; **12** 19

Sample B
Subtract

$$\begin{array}{r} 11 \\ \underline{-\ 4} \end{array}$$

○ 5
○ 6
○ 7
○ 15

STOP

7

$$\begin{array}{r} 19 \\ \underline{-\ 6} \end{array}$$

○ 6
○ 9
○ 12
○ 13

8

6 - 4 =

○ 2
○ 5
○ 8
○ 10

9

$$\begin{array}{r} 78 \\ \underline{-\ 76} \end{array}$$

○ 2
○ 12
○ 14
○ 18

10

$$\begin{array}{r} 147 \\ \underline{-\ 122} \end{array}$$

○ 19
○ 25
○ 29
○ 30

11

$$\begin{array}{r} 197 \\ \underline{-\ 68} \end{array}$$

○ 129
○ 135
○ 139
○ 140

12

$$\begin{array}{r} 202 \\ \underline{-\ 183} \end{array}$$

○ 19
○ 25
○ 75
○ 119

STOP

PLANNING NOTE

If you omitted Subtest 24, Multiplying and Dividing Numbers, on page 71, have students also omit items 13–18 on this page.

Read Aloud

In this part of the test, you will multiply or divide two numbers.

Put your finger on Sample C.

Read the numbers and the answer choices carefully. Then darken the circle next to the correct answer.

Give students time to do Sample C on their own. Then explain that 5 times 5 equals 25.

Now put your finger on Sample D.

Read the numbers and the answer choices carefully. Then darken the circle next to the correct answer.

Give students time to do Sample D on their own. Then explain that 16 divided by 4 equals 4.

Now put your finger on number 13. Do numbers 13 to 18 in the same way we did Sample C and Sample D. Notice whether the problem has a multiplication sign or a division sign in it.

Work until you reach the stop sign at the bottom of the page. Then put your pencils down.

Begin now.

Scratch Paper If you wish, give students practice in using scratch paper. Tell them to use the scratch paper to find their answers.

Answers: C 25; **D** 4; **13** 72; **14** 7; **15** 176; **16** 12; **17** 600; **18** 70

Sample C
Multiply

5 x 5 =

○ 10
○ 20
○ 25
○ 50

Sample D
Divide

16 ÷ 4 =

○ 3
○ 4
○ 8
○ 16

STOP

13

9 x 8 =

○ 56
○ 62
○ 64
○ 72

14

35 ÷ 5 =

○ 5
○ 6
○ 7
○ 15

15

$$\begin{array}{r} 22 \\ \underline{\times\ 8} \end{array}$$

○ 160
○ 166
○ 176
○ 186

16

96 ÷ 8 =

○ 9
○ 11
○ 12
○ 13

17

$$\begin{array}{r} 30 \\ \underline{\times\ 20} \end{array}$$

○ 60
○ 600
○ 6000
○ 6600

18

$3\overline{)210}$

○ 70
○ 71
○ 79
○ 707

Test 8

Mathmatical Concepts and Applications

Learn and Practice Strategies for Success

25. Understanding Numbers

Plan

Each problem is different. Tell yourself what each problem wants you to do.

Don't just guess. Think about the problem. Find a way to check your answer.

Find your own answer first. Then look for it in the answer choices.

Notice the two ways to list answer choices. Don't forget to check <u>all four</u> choices.

I know I can solve all these problems if I try my best.

To the Teacher *Please see the Planning Notes on pages 77, 84, and 87*

Scratch Paper If you wish, give students practice in using scratch paper. Tell them to use the scratch paper to find their answers.

Answers: A 8; 1 3; **2** 55, 60, 65, 70; **3** 1 dollar bill and 6 nickels

Do

Darken the circle next to the correct answer.

Sample A

Which number is missing from this pattern?
2, 4, 6, ___, 10

○ 6　　○ 8
○ 7　　○ 9

STOP

---

1 How many of the numbers in the box are greater than 100?

50	80	99	102	112	476

○ 3　　○ 5
○ 4　　○ 6

---

2 Which group of numbers shows counting by fives?

○ 16, 18, 22, 24
○ 27, 30, 33, 36
○ 40, 44, 48, 52
○ 55, 60, 65, 70

---

3 Ginny has 130 pennies. Which of these is the same amount of money?

○ 2 quarters, 1 dime, and 30 pennies
○ 1 dollar bill, 3 dimes, and 5 pennies
○ 1 dollar bill and 6 nickels
○ 4 quarters, 1 dime, and 7 pennies

GO ON

I'll keep asking myself this. What do I need to do to find the answer?

If I skip a question, I must make sure not to darken in any circles there.

4 Which number is greater than 5 and less than 12?

○ 3 ○ 14
○ 4 ○ 9

---

5 Which number tells how many blocks there are?

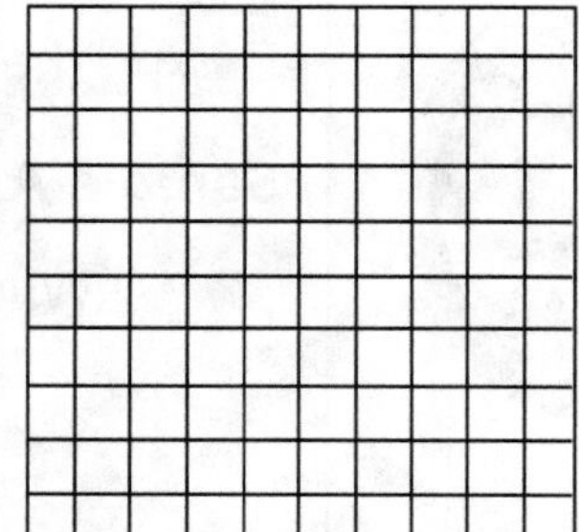

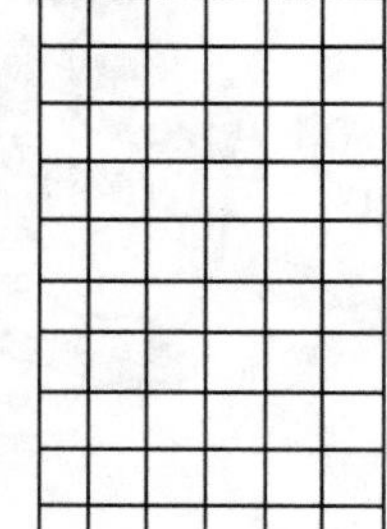

○ 136 ○ 361
○ 163 ○ 1,063

---

6 Which number has a 5 in the ones place, a 6 in the hundreds place, and a 9 in the tens place?

○ 596 ○ 695
○ 659 ○ 965

---

7 Which number comes next in this number pattern?

15, 12, 9, 6, ___

○ 5 ○ 1
○ 3 ○ 0

---

8 Which of these numbers would you use to estimate how much 93 – 48 is? Round to the nearest 10.

○ 95 and 50 ○ 90 and 50
○ 90 and 40 ○ 85 and 45

---

9 Which number has a 5 in the tens place?

○ 531 ○ 135
○ 315 ○ 55

STOP

Answers: 4 9; **5** 163; **6** 695; **7** 3; **8** 90 and 50; **9** 55

26. Solving Problems

Plan

Each problem is different. Tell yourself what each problem wants you to do.

Look for clues.
Should you add or subtract?
Should you multiply or divide?

Find your own answer first.
Then look for it in the answer choices.

Don't forget to check <u>all four</u> choices.

I'll take my time and think about each one.

PLANNING NOTE

Subtest 26, Solving Problems, is appropriate mainly for third grade students. If you teach students below grade 3, you may wish to skip pages 77–78.

Scratch Paper If you wish, give students practice in using scratch paper. Tell them to use the scratch paper to find their answers.

Answers: A $2.25; **1** 5; **2** 8; **3** Alice; **4** $3.75

Do

Darken the circle next to the correct answer.

Sample A

Max and Jeff have 75 cents. They need $1.50 more to buy what they want. How much does the thing they want to buy cost?

- ○ $2.00 ○ $2.50
- ○ $2.25 ○ $2.75

1 Which number makes this number sentence correct?

❑ + 12 = 17

- ○ 3 ○ 6
- ○ 5 ○ 8

2 Angela bought wheels for her in-line skates. Each skate has four wheels. How many wheels did she buy in all?

- ○ 4 ○ 8
- ○ 6 ○ 12

3 John is older than Marla and Ted. Alice is older than John. Who is the oldest of the four?

- ○ John ○ Ted
- ○ Marla ○ Alice

4 Len bought a slice of pizza for $1.25. He paid with a five-dollar bill. How much change did he get back?

- ○ $3.25 ○ $4.00
- ○ $3.75 ○ $4.75

GO ON

I'll make sure I know what the problem asks me to find.

I'll solve the problems on my own. Then I'll check the answer choices.

5 Which number makes this number sentence correct?

❑ - 12 = 12

○ 12 ○ 18
○ 15 ○ 24

---

6 There were 25 tropical fish in the tank. Then 10 of them were sold. How many tropical fish were left?

○ 10 ○ 35
○ 15 ○ 250

---

7 The store had 33 basketballs and 67 soccer balls in stock. How many balls in all did it have in stock?

○ 11 ○ 100
○ 44 ○ 480

---

8 Cindy had 24 stickers. She got 20 more as a gift. How many stickers did she have in all?

○ 4 ○ 64
○ 44 ○ 480

---

9 Which number makes both number sentences correct?

❑ - 4 = 4
❑ + 4 = 12

○ 4 ○ 12
○ 8 ○ 16

---

10 The fastest runner finished the race in 2 minutes. The slowest runner took 4 times as long to finish. How long did it take the slowest runner to finish?

○ 2 minutes ○ 8 minutes
○ 6 minutes ○ 10 minutes

STOP

Answers: 5 24; **6** 15; **7** 100; **8** 44; **9** 8; **10** 8 minutes

27. Using Graphs and Tables

Plan

Each problem is different. Tell yourself what each problem wants you to do.

In this test a few questions follow a chart or graph. Read the questions first. They will help you read the chart or graph with a purpose.

Don't forget to check <u>all four</u> choices.

If I change an answer, I'll erase everything in the circle.

Answers: A Donald; **1** Monday; **2** Wednesday; **3** Thursday and Friday

Do

Darken the circle next to the correct answer.

Sample A

Look at the graph. Which student has read the most books?

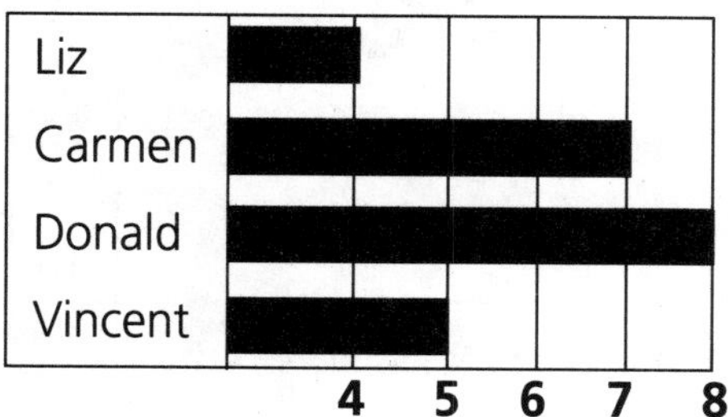

○ Liz ○ Carmen ○ Donald ○ Vincent

This chart shows the number of students absent in one school week. Study the chart. Then answer numbers 1–3.

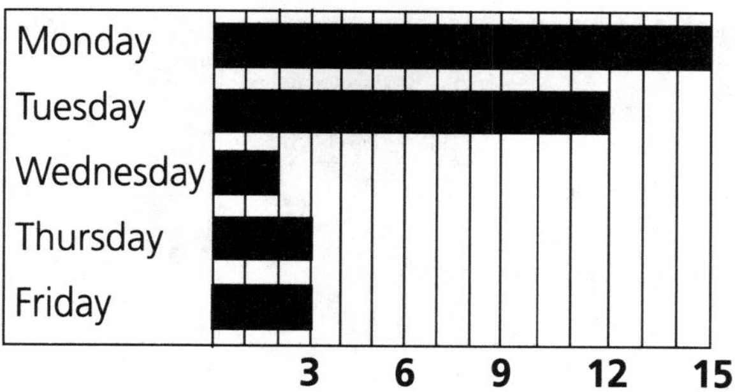

1 Which day had the most absences?

○ Monday ○ Wednesday
○ Tuesday ○ Friday

---

2 Which day had the fewest absences?

○ Tuesday ○ Thursday
○ Wednesday ○ Friday

---

3 Which two days have the same number of absences?

○ Monday and Tuesday
○ Tuesday and Wednesday
○ Wednesday and Thursday
○ Thursday and Friday

GO ON

If I skip a question, I shouldn't darken the answer circle for it.

This chart has lots of information. I'll read the questions first. I'll know what to look for.

PLANNING NOTE

The more complex graph and related test items on this page are appropriate mainly for third grade students. If you teach students below grade 3, you may wish to omit this part of Subtest 27.

Answers: 4 basketball; **5** swimming; **6** dodge ball; **7** 20; **8** skating and roller hockey

This graph shows the favorite after-school sports in one school. Study the graph. Then answer numbers 4–8.

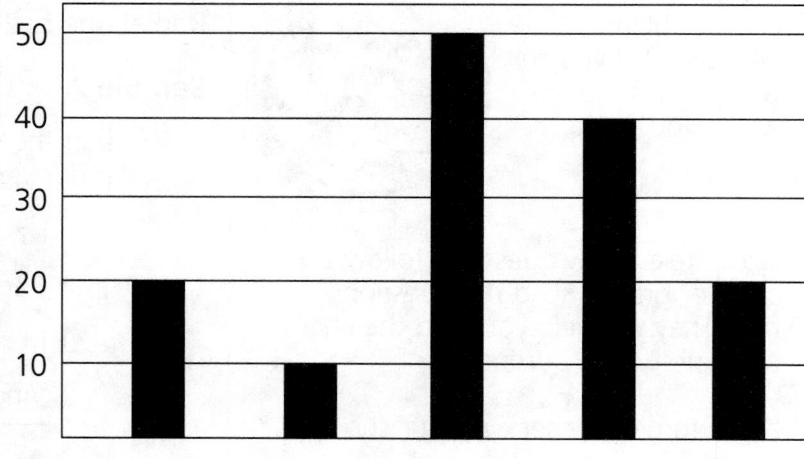

4 Which is the <u>most</u> popular after-school sport?

○ dodgeball ○ basketball
○ swimming ○ roller hockey

5 Which is the <u>second most popular</u> after-school sport?

○ skating ○ swimming
○ dodgeball ○ roller hockey

6 Which is the <u>least</u> popular after-school sport?

○ roller hockey ○ swimming
○ dodgeball ○ skating

7 How many students have roller hockey as their favorite sport?

○ 50 ○ 40
○ 30 ○ 20

8 What two sports are equally popular?

○ dodgeball and swimming
○ dodgeball and roller hockey
○ skating and roller hockey
○ skating and dodgeball

28. Using Time and Measurement

Plan

Remember to put the directions in your own words.

Think about Sample A. How does it help you understand what to do?

Look at each picture carefully. Tell yourself what the picture shows. If it's a clock face, read the time of day it shows.

If I change an answer, I'll erase everything in the circle.

Scratch Paper If you wish, give students practice in using scratch paper. Tell them to use the scratch paper to find their answers.

Answers: A 3:00 (bottom left clock face);
1 10:30; **2** 50 degrees; **3** 24 inches

Do

Darken the circle next to the correct answer.

Sample A

Which round clock face shows the same time as this digital watch face?

3:00

○ ○

○ ○

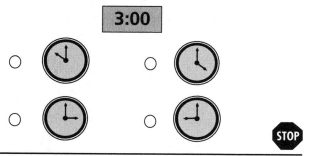

STOP

1 Which digital watch face shows the same time as this round clock face:

○ 7:00 ○ 10:30

○ 3:30 ○ 2:00

2 Which temperature does the thermometer show?

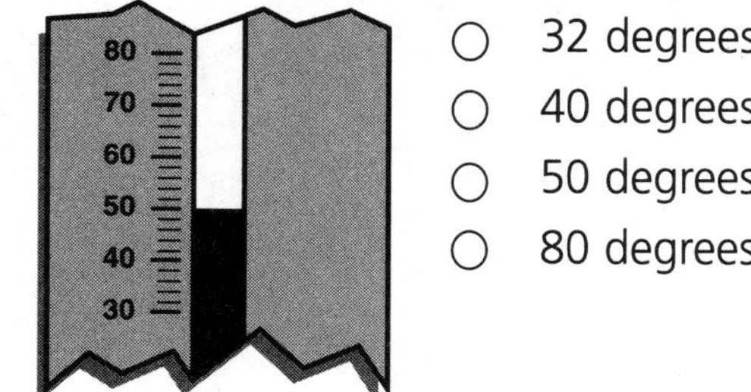

○ 32 degrees
○ 40 degrees
○ 50 degrees
○ 80 degrees

3 This ruler shows one foot or 12 inches. How many inches are there in 2 feet?

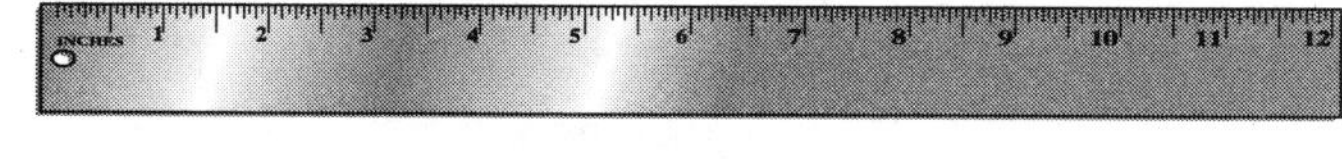

○ 12 inches ○ 24 inches

○ 18 inches ○ 36 inches

STOP

Mathematical Concepts and Applications

Time (optional): 50 minutes

Read Aloud

In this part of the test, you will solve problems that use numbers.

Put your finger on Sample A.

Read the problem and the answer choices carefully. Then darken the circle next to the correct answer.

Give students time to do Sample A on their own. Then explain that 2 dollar bills, 1 quarter, and 9 pennies equals 200 plus 25 plus 9 pennies, or $2.34.

Now put your finger on number 1. Do numbers 1 to 10 in the same way we did Sample A.

Work until you reach the stop sign at the bottom of the next page. Then put your pencils down.

Begin now.

Scratch Paper If you wish, give students practice in using scratch paper. Tell them to use the scratch paper to find their answers.

Answers: A 2 dollar bills, 1 quarter, and 9 pennies; **1** 16; **2** 91; **3** 52, 56, 60, 64; **4** 90 and 30

Sample A

Carla saved up 234 pennies. Which of these is the same amount of money?

- ○ 2 dollar bills, 1 quarter, and 9 pennies
- ○ 1 dollar bill, 4 quarters, and 3 dimes
- ○ 2 dollar bill, 7 nickels, and 4 pennies
- ○ 4 quarters, 1 dime, and seven pennies

1 Which number is missing from this pattern?

4, 8, 12, ___, 20

- ○ 4
- ○ 14
- ○ 16
- ○ 18

2 Which number is greater than 75 and less than 127?

- ○ 63
- ○ 91
- ○ 130
- ○ 142

3 Which group of numbers shows counting by fours?

- ○ 12, 16, 24, 30
- ○ 35, 40, 45, 50
- ○ 52, 56, 60, 64
- ○ 66, 69, 72, 75

4 Which of these numbers would you use to estimate how much 89 – 33 is? Round to the nearest 10.

- ○ 90 and 40
- ○ 100 and 30
- ○ 90 and 30
- ○ 90 and 35

GO ON

5 How many of the numbers in the box are greater than 330?

275	301	335	465	500	555

○ 2 ○ 4
○ 3 ○ 6

---

6 Which number has a 7 in the ones place, a 3 in the hundreds place, and a 5 in the tens place?

○ 375 ○ 53
○ 357 ○ 735

---

7 Which number has a 3 in the ones place?

○ 336 ○ 93
○ 39 ○ 30

---

8 Which number comes next in this number pattern?
25, 35, 45, 55, ___

○ 58 ○ 65
○ 60 ○ 70

---

9 Which number has a 5 in the tens place, a 7 in the ones place, and a 1 in the hundreds place?

○ 571 ○ 751
○ 175 ○ 157

---

10 Alan was the tenth boy to go outside for recess. How many boys went outside before him?

○ 8 ○ 10
○ 9 ○ 11

STOP

Answers: 5 4; **6** 357; **7** 93; **8** 65; **9** 157; **10** 9

Read Aloud

In this part of the test, you will solve number problems and word problems.

Put your finger on Sample B.

Read the problem and the answer choices carefully. Then darken the circle next to the correct answer.

Give students time to do Sample B on their own. Then explain that the problem is an addition problem. Which number added to 5 will give you 8? The answer is 3.

Now put your finger on number 11. Do numbers 11 to 21 in the same way we did Sample B.

Work until you reach the stop sign at the bottom of the next page. Then put your pencils down.

Begin now.

> **PLANNING NOTE**
>
> *If you omitted Subtest 26, Solving Problems, on pages 77–78, you should also omit test items 11–21 here on pages 84–85.*

Scratch Paper If you wish, give students practice in using scratch paper. Tell them to use the scratch paper to find their answers.

Answers: B 3; **11** 24; **12** 26; **13** $2.02; **14** 13; **15** 192

Sample B

Which number makes this number sentence correct?

❑ + 5 = 8

○ 3 ○ 6
○ 4 ○ 8

---

11 Iris had 29 stickers. She gave 5 to her best friend. How many stickers did Iris have left?

○ 19 ○ 25
○ 24 ○ 34

---

12 Anne needed 2 sticks of clay for every gift she made. She made 13 gifts. How many sticks of clay did she need?

○ 11 ○ 26
○ 15 ○ 28

---

13 Sara bought a pencil sharpener for $2.98. She paid with a five dollar bill. How much change did she get back?

○ $1.98 ○ $3.02
○ $2.02 ○ $3.20

---

14 There were 25 sandwiches on the tray. By noon 12 of them were sold. How many sandwiches were left?

○ 11 ○ 15
○ 13 ○ 37

---

15 The library sold 79 hardcover books and 113 softcover books. How many books in all did it sell?

○ 34 ○ 186
○ 182 ○ 192

GO ON

16 Ann and Beth have 50 cents. They need $1.25 more to buy a marker. How much does the marker they want cost?

- ○ $1.00
- ○ $1.75
- ○ $1.50
- ○ $2.25

---

17 Vera is taller than Sally and Kevin. Mimi is taller than Vera. Who is the tallest of the four?

- ○ Vera
- ○ Kevin
- ○ Sally
- ○ Mimi

---

18 Which number makes this number sentence correct?

❑ – 13 = 7

- ○ 14
- ○ 18
- ○ 16
- ○ 20

---

19 Louise bought a snack for $1.35. She paid with a one dollar bill and 2 quarters. How much change did she get back?

- ○ 15 cents
- ○ 55 cents
- ○ 20 cents
- ○ 65 cents

---

20 Which number makes both number sentences correct?

❑ – 6 = 7
❑ + 3 = 16

- ○ 9
- ○ 13
- ○ 11
- ○ 15

---

21 The fastest car finished the race in 12 minutes. The slowest car took 3 times as long to finish. How long did it take the slowest car to finish?

- ○ 4 minutes
- ○ 30 minutes
- ○ 24 minutes
- ○ 36 minutes

STOP

Answers: 16 $1.75; **17** Mimi; **18** 20; **19** 15 cents; **20** 13; **21** 36 minutes

Read Aloud

In this part of the test, you will solve problems using charts and graphs.

Put your finger on Sample C.

Read the problem and the answer choices carefully. Then darken the circle next to the correct answer.

Give students time to do Sample C on their own. Then explain that the chart shows that Maria won eight stars, and that is the most shown on the chart for any one person.

Now put your finger on number 22. Do numbers 22 to 29 in the same way we did Sample C.

Work until you reach the stop sign at the bottom of the next page. Then put your pencils down.

Begin now.

Scratch Paper If you wish, give students practice in using scratch paper. Tell them to use the scratch paper to find their answers.

Answers: C Maria; **22** 48 inches; **23** 9; **24** 15

Sample C

Look at the graph. Which student has won the most stars?

Maria	★★★★★★★★
Magda	★★★★★★
Carlos	★★★★★★★
Hakim	★★★★★★★

○ Maria ○ Magda ○ Carlos ○ Hakim

This chart shows how tall students in one class are. Study the chart. Then answer numbers 22–24.

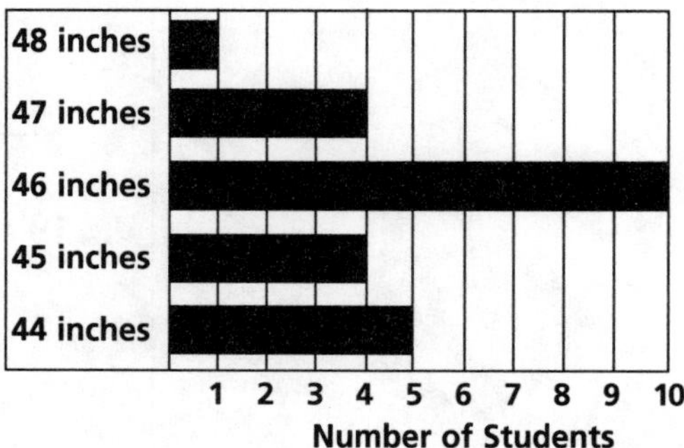

22 How tall is the tallest person in the class?

○ 45 inches ○ 47 inches
○ 46 inches ○ 48 inches

23 How many people are 45 inches tall or less?

○ 4 ○ 9
○ 5 ○ 10

24 How many people are 46 inches tall or more?

○ 5 ○ 15
○ 14 ○ 19

PLANNING NOTE

If you omitted the more complex graph and test items in Subtest 27, page 80, because the students you teach are not yet in grade 3, you may also wish to skip questions 25–29 on this page.

Answers: 25 dry cereal; **26** pancakes; **27** eggs and muffins; **28** 50; **29** 60

This graph shows the favorite breakfast foods of third graders. Study the graph. Then answer numbers 25–29.

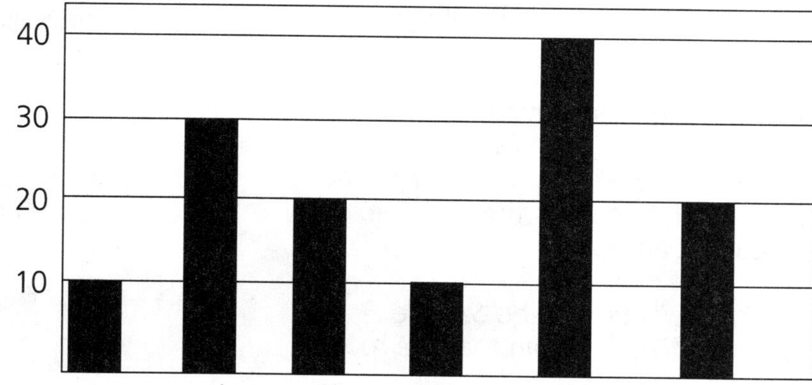

25 Which is the <u>most</u> popular breakfast food?

- ○ eggs ○ dry cereal
- ○ pancakes ○ hot cereal

---

26 Which is the <u>second most popular</u> breakfast food?

- ○ pancakes ○ muffins
- ○ waffles ○ hot cereal

---

27 Which are the two <u>least</u> popular breakfast foods?

- ○ muffins and hot cereal
- ○ eggs and hot cereal
- ○ waffles and dry cereal
- ○ eggs and muffins

---

28 How many students ate either pancakes or waffles?

- ○ 20 ○ 40
- ○ 30 ○ 50

---

29 How many students preferred cereal, either dry or hot?

- ○ 60 ○ 40
- ○ 50 ○ 30

STOP

Read Aloud

In this part of the test, you will solve problems that involve time and measurement.

Put your finger on Sample D.

Read the problem and the answer choices carefully. Then darken the circle next to the correct answer.

Give students time to do Sample D on their own. Then explain that the round clock face reads 3:00.

Now put your finger on number 30. Do numbers 30 to 32 in the same way we did Sample D.

Work until you reach the stop sign at the bottom of the page. Then put your pencils down.

Begin now.

Scratch Paper If you wish, give students practice in using scratch paper. Tell them to use the scratch paper to find their answers.

Answers: D 3:00; **30** 7:00 (top left clock face); **31** 9 feet; **32** 70 degrees

Sample D

Which digital watch face shows the same time as this round clock face:

○ 11:00 ○ 11:30

○ 3:00 ○ 1:00

STOP

30 Which round clock face shows the same time as this digital watch?

7:00

○ ○

○ ○

31 Look at the yardstick below. How many feet are there in 3 yards?

○ 3 feet ○ 9 feet

○ 6 feet ○ 12 feet

32 What temperature does the thermometer show?

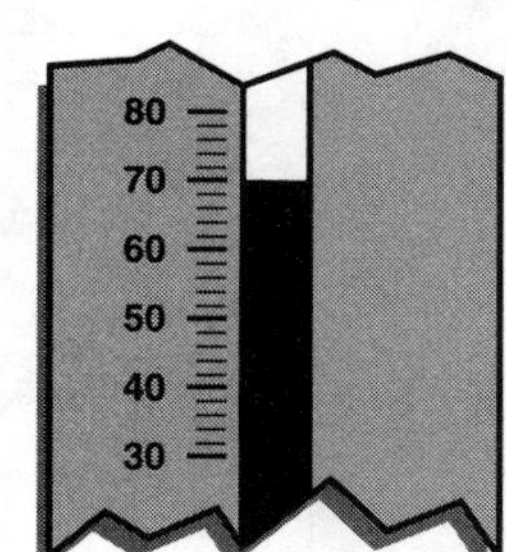

○ 32 degrees

○ 40 degrees

○ 70 degrees

○ 80 degrees

Reference and Study Skills

Learn and Practice Strategies for Success

29. Using a Dictionary Entry

Plan

Read for a purpose. Before you read the entry, read the questions. Know what you are looking for.

Read all the answer choices before you pick.

Stay focused. Watch out for choices that are meant to throw you off track.

There's only one dictionary entry. It must be for all the questions.

PLANNING NOTE

The California Achievement Test (CAT) and the Comprehensive Test of Basic Skills (CTBS) do not test reference and study skills at grade 3 or below. If you are preparing your students to take either of these tests, you may omit all parts of Test 9, pages 89–94.

Answers: A climbing; **1** the first word and the last word on the dictionary page; **2** how to pronounce the word

Do

Darken the circle next to the correct answer.

Sample A

Clerk • Clock

clerk (klerk) person who works in a store to sell goods
cliff (klif) a very steep slope of rock
cliff dwelling cave or house built on a cliff
cliff-hanger *informal* a very suspenseful story
climb (klīm) **climbed**, **climbing** to use the hands and feet to go up

How do you spell <u>climb</u> when you add -<u>ing</u> to it?

- ○ climbed
- ○ climming
- ○ climing
- ○ climbing

---

1 What do the words **Clerk • Clock** at the top of the page tell you?

- ○ the first word and the last word on the dictionary page
- ○ the spelling of the two most important words on the page.
- ○ the two most interesting entries on the page
- ○ the two hardest to spell words on the page

---

2 What does (klif) in the entry for <u>cliff</u> tell you?

- ○ how to spell the word
- ○ what a second spelling of the word is
- ○ how to pronounce the word
- ○ how use the word in a sentence

STOP

30. Using the Parts of a Book

Plan

Read for a purpose. Before you read the entry, read the questions. Know what you are looking for.

Read all the answer choices before you pick.

Stay focused. Watch out for choices that are meant to throw you off track.

There's only one table of contents. It must be for all the questions.

Do

Darken the circle next to the correct answer.

Sample A

Book Title: *Water Birds*

Contents

Canada Goose............ 3
Mallard....................... 5
Kingfisher.................... 7
Grebe......................... 8
Whooping Crane.........11
Heron.........................13
Flamingo....................15
Loon...........................18
Puffin........................ 20

How many chapters are in the book *Water Birds*?

- ○ 6 chapters
- ○ 8 chapters
- ○ 9 chapters
- ○ 10 chapters

1 On which page does information about herons begin?

- ○ page 3
- ○ page 5
- ○ page 13
- ○ page 20

2 Is this a good book to use to find out more about swans?

- ○ Yes, I'd look on page 3.
- ○ Yes, I'd look on page 5.
- ○ Yes, I'd look on page 18.
- ○ No, swans are not listed in the contents.

Answers: A 9 chapters; **1** page 13; **2** No, swans are not listed in the contents.

31. Using the Library

Plan

Tell yourself what you need to do. Put the directions in your own words.

Read all the answers before you pick.

Skip questions you can't answer. Come back to them later.

Stay focused. Think about the questions. Watch out for choices that are meant to throw you off track.

I'll tell myself what I can find in each kind of book.

Answers: A Biography; **1** a map of a country; **2** a book about health; **3** by checking the copyright date

Do

Darken the circle next to the correct answer.

Sample A

Which section of the library would have a book about famous baseball players?

- ○ Fiction
- ○ Biography
- ○ Humor
- ○ Travel

---

1 Which of these would you find in an atlas?

- ○ a map of a country
- ○ a short story about a country
- ○ a play about a country
- ○ recipes from the country

---

2 Which of these books will probably tell you how to bandage a cut?

- ○ a music book
- ○ a book about social studies
- ○ a book about health
- ○ a math book

---

3 How can you tell if the information in a book is up-to-date?

- ○ by looking at the illustrations
- ○ by checking the color of the paper it's printed on
- ○ by checking the copyright date
- ○ by looking for the word New in the title

Reference and Study Skills

Time (optional): 20 minutes

Read Aloud

In this part of the test, you will answer questions about dictionary entries.

Put your finger on Sample A.

Read the dictionary entry and the questions carefully. Then darken the circle next to the correct answer.

Give students time to do Sample A on their own. Then explain that the part of the entry that follows the main entry word often tells you how to pronounce it.

Now put your finger on number 1. Do numbers 1 and 2 in the same way we did Sample A. Use the dictionary entry in Sample A.

Work until you reach the stop sign at the bottom of the page. Then put your pencils down.

Begin now.

Answers: A the pronunciation; **1** fuel; **2** The phrase has a special meaning in basketball.

Sample A

free • freeway

free (frē) not under another person's control
freebooter a pirate, a buccaneer
freehand done by hand without using a ruler or other device
free throw (in basketball) an open, unblocked shot at the basket awarded to a player who has been fouled
freeway (frē′ wā) a high-speed highway on which tolls are not charged

What does (frē) in the entry for <u>free</u> tell you?

- ○ the pronunciation
- ○ the spelling
- ○ the kind of word it is
- ○ the meaning

STOP

---

1 Which of the following words will you <u>not</u> find on this dictionary page?

- ○ freedom
- ○ fuel
- ○ frisk
- ○ fresh

---

2 Why does the entry for <u>free throw</u> have the note (in basketball)?

- ○ Dictionaries are books about sports.
- ○ The phrase has a special meaning in basketball.
- ○ It tells a special pronunciation of the word in basketball.
- ○ It tells other forms of the word.

Read Aloud

In this part of the test, you will answer questions about a table of contents.

Put your finger on Sample B.

Read the table of contents and the answer choices carefully. Then darken the circle next to the correct answer.

Give students time to do Sample B on their own. Then explain that all of the entries below the word Contents *are chapter titles.*

Now put your finger on number 3. Do numbers 3 to 5 in the same way we did Sample B. Use the table of contents in Sample B to answer the questions.

Work until you reach the stop sign at the bottom of the page. Then put your pencils down.

Begin now.

Answers: B 8; **3** the page on which the chapter starts; **4** page 9; **5** No, this book is only about desert animals.

Sample B

Book Title: *Desert Animals*

Contents

Antelope Jackrabbit.... 5
Kangaroo Rat............. 7
Coyote...................... 9
Roadrunner................ 10
Horned Lizard............ 13
Gila Monster.............. 14
Scorpion.................... 17
Sidewinder................. 18

How many chapter titles do you find in the book *Desert Animals*?

- ○ 2
- ○ 4
- ○ 6
- ○ 8

STOP

3 What do the numbers on the right-hand side of the table of contents show?

- ○ the number of pages in the chapter
- ○ the number of animals the chapter talks about
- ○ the page on which the chapter starts
- ○ the number of pages left until the end of the book

4 On which page would you expect to find information about coyotes?

- ○ page 5
- ○ page 9
- ○ page 7
- ○ page 17

5 Is this a good book to look in for information about polar bears?

- ○ Yes, I would look on page 7.
- ○ Yes, I would look on page 10.
- ○ Yes, I would look on page 14.
- ○ No, this book is only about desert animals.

STOP

Read Aloud

In this part of the test, you will answer questions about using books in the library.

Put your finger on Sample C. Read the question and the answer choices carefully. Then darken the circle next to the correct answer.

Give students time to do Sample C on their own. Then explain that the stars are a technical subject that would probably be discussed in a science book.

Now put your finger on number 6. Do numbers 6 to 9 in the same way we did Sample C.

Work until you reach the stop sign at the bottom of the page. Then put your pencils down.

Begin now.

Answers: C a science book; **6** the sports and recreation section; **7** a long article about a country; **8** Fiction; **9** Arts and Crafts

Sample C

Which of these books will probably tell you about the stars?

- ○ a cookbook
- ○ a book about railroads
- ○ a social studies book
- ○ a science book

6 In which section of the library would you first look to find a book about roller hockey?

- ○ The Arts/Music
- ○ Science
- ○ Social studies
- ○ Sports and Recreation

7 Which of these would you find in an encyclopedia?

- ○ a long article about a country
- ○ a short story about a country
- ○ current events taking place in a country
- ○ only a one- or two-line entry about a country

8 Which section of the library would have a novel about the adventures of two grade-school friends?

- ○ Fiction
- ○ Biography
- ○ Social Studies
- ○ Travel

9 Which section of the library would have a book about making greeting cards?

- ○ Fiction
- ○ Arts and Crafts
- ○ Technology
- ○ Geography

Alternative Assessment Strategies

The computerized reports that test-makers provide to record the results of standardized testing give teachers and schools an extensive portrait of student achievement. But even the most vocal advocates of standardized testing will agree that these reports do not provide a total portrait of what students have accomplished. For this kind of data, teachers nationwide are turning toward alternative forms of assessment. The most widespread of these forms is portfolio assessment.

What Is Portfolio Assessment?

Portfolio assessment documents student achievement over time. First developed to gauge students' growth as writers, portfolio assessment has grown beyond collecting writing samples to encompass written works and other projects developed in all content areas. Portfolios can include artwork, videotapes, audiotapes, science experiments, and other forms of personal and intellectual expression—whatever teacher and student agree should be in the portfolio.

Choice and Who Chooses

The hallmark of portfolio assessment is choice. Early in the year, students and teachers discuss what a portfolio is and how they will go about compiling theirs.

- The teacher and student decide together what should be in the portfolio. Will it be only the student's best work? Will it be finished works only or should it also present works in progress? Should there be a required number of works in the portfolio by year's end, as a goal for students to aim toward, or will contents reflect the pace of each student's learning? These and many other questions specific to a teacher's class room must be addressed and resolved early in the year.
- Of great importance in a program of portfolio evaluation is who chooses the items that go into the portfolio. Ideally, the choice is the student's. The process helps develop the student's sense of ownership of what he or she is learning. The student becomes more actively involved in and responsible for learning and for recognizing when his or her work has improved.
- Standards are also important. At the start of the year, teachers and students need to work together to develop criteria for the level of work that will go into a portfolio.

  For written work, the teacher may want students to include a "baseline sample" against which students can measure their progress over the course of the year.

Advantages of Portfolio Assessment for the Teacher

Because the process of portfolio assessment encourages ongoing communication about projects and progress, teachers have more opportunities than conventional assessment methods allow to identify a learner's strengths and weaknesses and thereby individualize learning.

The portfolio itself is an excellent means to show parents during teacher conferences how their children are performing in school. Parents see more than a grade. They see growth and progress in a concrete, tangible form. Teachers may also use contents of the portfolio to discuss students' work with administrators, counselors, and other teachers.

Teachers who plan to adopt portfolio assessment as an evaluation tool should communicate with parents their plans for the year and build an understanding of how portfolio assessment works. Parents will see for themselves the benefits it affords their children's education.